CRISt

THE MEANING OF THE
TWENTIETH CENTURY
The Great Transition

THE MEANING OF THE TWENTIETH CENTURY

The Great Transition

KENNETH E. BOULDING

HARPER COLOPHON BOOKS
HARPER & ROW, PUBLISHERS
NEW YORK

This Colophon paperback edition reprints Volume XXXIV of the World Perspectives Series, which is planned and edited by Ruth Nanda Anshen. Dr. Anshen's Epilogue to this reprint appears on page 203.

THE MEANING OF THE TWENTIETH CENTURY: The Great Transition. Copyright © 1964 by Kenneth Ewart Boulding. Printed in the United States of America. All rights reserved. No part of this book may be used or reproduced in any manner whatsoever without written permission except in the case of brief quotations embodied in critical articles and reviews. For information address Harper & Row, Publishers, Incorporated, 49 East 33rd Street, New York, N.Y. 10016.

First Harper Colophon edition published 1965 by Harper & Row, Publishers, Incorporated, New York.

Library of Congress Catalog Card Number: 64-20540

Contents

Contents

I.

The Great Transition

THE twentieth century marks the middle period of a great transition in the state of the human race. It may properly be called the second great transition in the history of mankind.

The first transition was that from precivilized to civilized society which began to take place about five (or ten) thousand years ago.* This is a transition that is still going on in some parts of the world, although it can be regarded as almost complete. Precivilized society can now be found only in small and rapidly diminishing pockets in remote areas. It is doubtful whether more than 5 per cent of the

---

* The first transition falls into two parts, the transition from the paleolithic to the neolithic, following the invention of agriculture, and the subsequent transition from the neolithic village to urban civilization. I prefer to think of these two parts as parts of a single process, but some may prefer to regard them as two separate transitions, in which case the modern transition would be the "third." See p. 29.

world's population could now be classified as living in a genuinely precivilized society.

Even as the first great transition is approaching completion, however, a second great transition is treading on its heels. It may be called the transition from civilized to postcivilized society. We are so accustomed to giving the word civilization a favorable overtone that the words postcivilized or postcivilization may strike us as implying something unfavorable. If, therefore, the word technological or the term developed society is preferred I would have no objection. The word postcivilized, however, does bring out the fact that civilization is an intermediate state of man dividing the million or so years of precivilized society from an equally long or longer period which we may expect to extend into the future postcivilization. It is furthermore a rather disagreeable state for most people living in it, and its disappearance need occasion few tears.

The origins of the first great transition from precivilized society are lost in the mists of prehistory except in so far as they can be reconstructed with the aid of archeology. The more we know the further these origins seem to recede in time, and it now seems clear that the beginning of agriculture and the domestication of animals can be traced back at least ten thousand years. Agriculture is a precondition of the development of civilization because it is not until man settles down and begins to cultivate crops and domesticate livestock that he is able to develop a surplus of food from the food producer above and beyond what the food producer and his family require themselves for their own maintenance. In hunting, fishing, and pastoral societies it seems to have been hard for the food producer to produce much more than the immediate requirements of himself and his family. In these circumstances it is clear that no urban culture can possibly exist. If persons who do not produce food are to be fed, there must be surplus food available from the food producer. Some precivilized societies seem to have enjoyed such a surplus, but it was always precarious and temporary. There must be a continuous and reasonably stable excess of food production above the requirements of the food producer if civilization is to be established.

The mere existence of surplus food, while it is a prerequisite for the existence of civilization, does not necessarily produce it, for surplus may be "wasted" in leisure or unproductive activities. In order for towns and cities to exist there must be some machinery whereby the food surplus of the food producer is extracted from him and collected in one place so that the kings, priests, soldiers, builders, and artisans of civilization can subsist. I am assuming here that the prime mark of civilization is the city. This is indeed what the derivation of the word civilization suggests. In its earliest form the city seems to have been a product of some system of coercion. Agriculture provides the opportunity, but in the early stages at least it seems to take some form of coercion to take advantage of it. The earliest forms of coercion may well have been spiritual, for there is some evidence that the earliest cities were organized as theocracies. A priesthood arises which claims a monopoly on the supposedly supernatural forces which govern the affairs of man and the fertility of crops and livestock. The priest then is able to extract food from the food producer by threatening to deprive him of the assistance of these supernatural forces. The coercive system of the priest, however, is based to a large extent on bluff, for the priest does not really control the forces that make the crops grow. When the priest ceases to inspire belief in his imaginary powers the spiritual coercive system usually seems to be replaced by a more physical coercive system in the shape of a king and army. In isolation this is a fairly stable system because when the king has sufficient means of violence at his disposal he can threaten the food producer enough to make him give up his surplus. With this food surplus the king can feed his army and so reinforce the threat if necessary. With what is left over from feeding the army, the king can feed architects, builders, priests, philosophers, and other adornments of civilization. In this stage an alliance is frequently made between the king and the priest, and physical and spiritual threats reinforce each other. The economic basis on which classical civilization has been built, however, has universally been meager. Whether it was Sumeria, Egypt, Greece, Rome, Ancient China, the Incas, or the Mayans, all these were societies based on a food surplus from the food producer that rarely exceeded 20 or 25 per cent of the total product. In these circumstances three quarters to four fifths of the population must be in agriculture or other food production, and these people barely produce enough to feed the remaining quarter or fifth of the population in the towns and in the army. Almost all the cities of classical civilization were within a few weeks of starvation at any time, and a relatively small worsening in general conditions, in the means of transportation or in conditions of peace and war, was frequently enough to undermine the precarious foundation of civilized life. I have never seen any figure for the expectation of life of the city itself under conditions of classical civilization, but I would be surprised if this turned out to be more than about three hundred years.

The origins of the second great transition are perhaps not so obscure as the origins of the first but there are many puzzling and unresolved questions connected with them. All through the history of civilization, indeed, one can detect a slowly rising stream of knowledge and organization that has a different quality from that of the civilized society around it. The astronomy of Babylonia, the geometry of the Greeks, and the algebra of the Arabs represent as it were foretastes of the great flood of knowledge and technological change to come. Some of the ancient empires, even the Roman Empire, seem to have been technologically stagnant and scientifically backward. If one is looking for the beginning of a continuous process of scientific and technological development this might be traced to the monastic movement in the West of the sixth century A.D., especially the Benedictines. Here for almost the first time in history we had intellectuals who worked with their hands, and who belonged to a religion which regarded the physical world as in some sense sacred and capable of enshrining goodness. It is not surprising therefore that an interest in the economizing of labor and in extending its productive powers began in the monasteries, however slowly. From the sixth century on we can trace a slowly expanding technology. The water wheel comes in the sixth century, the stirrup in the eighth, the horse collar and the rudder in the ninth, the windmill in the twelfth, and so on. For Europe the invention of printing in the fifteenth century represents an irreversible take-off, because from this point on the dissemination of information increased with great rapidity. The seventeenth century saw the beginning of science, the eighteenth century an acceleration of technological change so great that it has been called, perhaps rather misleadingly, the Industrial Revolution. The nineteenth century saw the development of science as an ongoing social organization, and the twentieth century has seen research and development heavily institutionalized with an enormous increase in the rate of change both of knowledge and of technology as a result. It must be emphasized that the rate of change still seems to be accelerating. We may not even have reached the middle of whatever process we are passing through, and there are certainly no signs that the rate of change is slowing down. It seems clear for instance that we are now on the edge of a biological revolution which may have results for mankind just as dramatic as the nuclear revolution of a generation ago.

A few symptoms will indicate the magnitude of the change through which we are now passing. Consider for instance the position of agriculture in the most developed societies today. In all societies of classical civilizaton, as we have seen, at least 75 per cent of the population, and often a larger percentage, were engaged in agriculture and would merely produce enough to support themselves and the remaining urban 25 per cent. Even in the United States at the time of the American Revolution, it has been estimated that about 90 per cent of the people were in agriculture. Today in the United States only about 10 per cent of the population are so engaged, and if present trends continue it will not be long before we can produce all the food that we need with 5 per cent, or even less, of the population. This is because with modern techniques, a single farmer and his family can produce enough food to feed ten, twenty, or even thirty families. This releases more than 90 per cent of the population to work on other things, and to produce automobiles, houses, clothing, all the luxuries and conveniences of life as well as missiles and nuclear weapons.

Another indication of the magnitude of the present transition is the fact that, as far as many statistical series related to activities of mankind are concerned, the date that divides human history into two equal parts is well within living memory. For the volume and number of chemical publications, for instance, this date is now (*i.e.* 1964) about 1950. For many statistical series of quantities of metal or other materials extracted, this date is about 1910. That is, man took about as much out of mines before 1910 as he did after 1910. Another startling fact is that about 25 per cent of the human beings who have ever lived are now alive, and what is even more astonishing, something like 90 per cent of all the scientists who have ever lived are now alive. My eight-year-old son asked me the other day, "Daddy, were you born in the olden days?" It is the sort of question that makes a parent feel suddenly middle-aged. There is perhaps more truth in his remark than he knew. In a very real sense the changes in the state of mankind since the date of my birth have been greater than the changes that took place in many thousands of years before this date.

Another indication of the magnitude of the transition is the extraordinary ability of modern societies to recover from disaster. In 1945, for instance, many of the cities of Germany and Japan lay in almost total ruin. Today it is hard to tell that they were ever destroyed, for they have been completely rebuilt in a space of less than twenty years. It took Western Europe almost three hundred years to recover from the fall of the Roman Empire, and it took Germany decades to recover from the Thirty Years War (1618–1648). It is perhaps an optimistic feature of the present time that as well as great powers of destruction, we also have greatly increased powers of recuperation and recovery.

The great transition is not only something that takes place in science, technology, the physical machinery of society, and in the utilization of physical energy. It is also a transition in social institutions. Changes in technology produce change in social institutions, and changes in institutions produce change in technology. In the enormously complex world of social interrelations we cannot say in any simple way that one change produces the other, only that they are enormously interrelated and both aspects of human life change together. For instance, it has been argued that the invention of the rudder and the improvement in the arts of navigation and shipbuilding which took place in Europe in the fifteenth century led inevitably to the discovery of America by Europeans. As a schoolboy is reported to have said, "How could Columbus miss it?" Once it was possible to navigate a course of three thousand miles in a straight line, the discovery of America by the Europeans was virtually inevitable, and of course this discovery enormously expanded the horizon and the opportunities of these European societies.

On the other hand, the societies which pioneered in the discovery of America did not ultimately profit very much from it. Spain and Portugal obtained a great empire and a sizable inflation but stagnated as a result, because of the failure of their social institutions to adapt.

It has likewise been argued that the discovery of the horse collar eventually led to the abolition of slavery, at least in its more extreme forms, because of the fact that with a horse collar the horse became a much more efficient source of mere animal power than a human, and the slave as a simple source of power could not compete with him. A horse collar seems to be such an obvious invention that one can hardly believe that it took until the ninth century for mankind to think of it. However, it seems to be clear that the Romans did not use it, and that the Roman horse pulled on rope that was something like a noose around its neck, which greatly reduced its efficiency. The horse collar, coupled with the development of the three-field system, led to a substantial improvement in the techniques of agriculture in Europe in the ninth, tenth, and eleventh centuries which was the foundation on which the cultural and architectural achievements of the later Middle Ages were built. Here again, however, the social institutions of its feudal and authoritarian societies led to a freezing of the technological situation, and further advance in agriculture did not come until the institutions of the Middle Ages had largely disintegrated or at least were weakened through the inflation which followed on the inflow of the Spanish gold from the New World. The rise of Protestantism and the breakup of the old transitional society produced a situation in Holland and in England in which innovation was once more possible, and the agricultural revolution of the seventeenth and early eighteenth centuries grew out of the developing of root crops, the use of intertilled crops on previously fallow ground, and the sowing of artificial grasses. This improvement in agriculture, at least in England and the Low Countries in the early eighteenth century, laid the foundation for a growing food surplus for the industrial cities to come.

The social invention of parliamentary democracy permitted societies to develop with much greater diversity and wider distribution of power that in the earlier absolute monarchies, and the rise of modern science is quite closely associated with the development of democratic and pluralistic institutions of this kind. It could not arise, for instance, in imperial China or feudal Japan. It is no accident that an acceleration in the growth of science took place in Western Europe following the French Revolution. It is clear that we must look at pure science, technological change, and social invention as parts of a single pattern of development in which each element supports the other. It may be argued indeed that social institutions play more of a negative than a positive role, in that they can inhibit scientific and technological change but cannot initiate it. Even this proposition, however, must now be called in question. Organized research and development is essentially a social invention which has resulted in an enormous increase in the pace of technological change.

As another example of the interrelation of technical and political change it can be argued, for instance, that it is the progress of technology, especially under the stimulus of organized research and development, that has effectively abolished imperialism. Ancient civilization, as we have seen, rested firmly on a basis of coercion. The food producer had to be coerced into giving up the surplus to king or priest because there was nothing much that either of them produced that could be exchanged for it. The ancient city is to a large extent an instrument of exploitation and must be regarded as parasitic on the food producer. In the modern world things are different. Since the development of industrial society, exchange has replaced coercion as the principal means of social organization even though coercion and the threat of violence still retain a great importance in the relations of national states. But with the coming of science and technology, it is fair to say that we can get ten dollars out of nature for every dollar that we can squeeze out of man. Under these circumstances imperial adventure or political coercion is simply an investment with a much lower rate of return than investment in applied science and technological progress at home. We see this very clearly, for instance, in the case of Portugal, which now has probably the largest *per capita* empire and the lowest *per capita* income in Europe. By contrast, the Scandinavian countries and Switzerland, which have refrained from imperial adventures, have probably done better economically than their more imperial counterparts. The progressive abandonment of empire by the British, the French, the Dutch, and the Belgians reflects not so much a power shift on the part of these countries as their recognition that in terms of the values of a modern society, empire simply does not pay

Social inventions often take place so softly and imperceptibly that they are hardly noticed, and the history of social invention as a result still largely remains to be written. Who for instance invented the handshake? How did we change from a society in which almost every man went armed to a society in which we have achieved almost complete personal disarmament, and in which human relations are governed by conventions of politeness, by disarming methods of communication, and by largely nonviolent techniques of conflict? Most of all, how do changes take place in child rearing? These perhaps are the most fundamental social inventions of all, for the personality structure of one generation depends mainly on the way children were brought up in the previous generation.

As part of the ongoing process of social invention the great transition involves changes in moral, religious, and aesthetic aspects of life just as much as it involves changes in our knowledge and use of the physical world. It involves, for instance, change in the nature of the family and in the patterns of child rearing. Civilized society on the whole is characterized by the extended family, and by strong loyalty to kinfolk and by methods of child rearing which generally involve a rough transition from an extremely permissive and protective early childhood to an authoritarian and unpleasant regime in later childhood. As we move to postcivilized society, we find an extension of loyalty from the kinship group to larger areas such as the national state, or even to the world as a whole. The family structure and

living arrangement tend to shift from the extended family
group and large household to the small nuclear family of
parents and children, and we find that the child-rearing
practices which may be well adapted to a society in which
the threat systems are important and aggression pays off,
have become poorly adapted to a society in which the
subtler arts of personal manipulation replace the more
violent forms of aggression. We therefore find a shift in the
methods of child rearing from those which produce the
authoritarian personalities which are characteristic of civilized societies to those which produce more flexible, adaptable, and manipulative persons.

Drastic changes in the nature and behavior of the family
are also implied by the health revolution which is also a
part of the transition. In civilized society, mortality is high
and there is a necessity therefore for a high birth rate.
Civilized society can be in equilibrium with birth and
death rates between thirty and forty per thousand and a
corresponding expectation of life between thirty-three and
twenty-five. It is a matter of simple arithmetic that in an
equilibrium population in which birth rate and death rate
are equal, the level of the birth and death rates is the simple
reciprocal of the average age at death. In the advanced societies today the average age at death is about seventy, and
for such a population to be in equilibrium the birth and
death rate must be about fourteen. To put the matter in
somewhat different terms, if all children live to maturity
and if the whole population marries, then the average num-

ber of children in one family cannot exceed two, if population is to be stable. This also implies no more than an average of two births per family. This involves an enormous shift in attitude toward children and even perhaps toward sex. Yet this is an essential part of the transition. If this part of the transition is not made, all the rest cannot be made either, except as a temporary and unstable condition.

The great transition likewise involves a profound change in the nature of religion and ideology. In a society in which religion is associated with animistic views of the universe and with a belief in magic, the behavior changes which are necessary to the great transition can hardly take place. If man believes that natural objects like stones, wind, water, and crops are moved by essentially arbitrary wills, either he will despair of manipulating nature to his own advantage or he will attempt to do this in the same way that he would attempt to manipulate his fellow man—that is, by attempts at verbal or symbolic communication, in the form of incantation and ritual. It is not until animism is replaced by an attitude which regards will as essentially and solely a property of the minds and souls of men, rather than of inanimate natural objects, that a scientific and technological attitude toward the material world becomes possible. It is no accident therefore that the scientific transition originated in Western Europe, where the prevailing religion was an ethical monotheism, which either tended to concentrate the whole animistic enterprise in a single sacramental act of the Mass, as in Catholic Christianity, or which denied even this apparent remnant of animism by stressing that the operation of the will of God takes place principally in the souls of men, as in Protestant Christianity.

We may even attribute the success of atheistic communism in promoting economic development and the movement toward postcivilized society not so much to its specific dogmas as to the fact that it is an instrument for undermining primitive animism and for replacing a belief in the arbitrary and willful nature of the material world by a belief in its stability and orderliness. Whether this view can ultimately satisfy the spiritual needs of man is another question altogether. It is clear that the scientific and technological transition is consistent with many different views about the ultimate nature of the universe, provided that they all involve a faith in the orderliness of the natural world, faith in man's ability to perceive this order and manipulate it for his own benefit, and faith in processes of learning which involve direct experience rather than mere acceptance of the received tradition from the elders.

The various civilizations which resulted from the first great transition, even though they had much in common, nevertheless exhibited great differences. One needs merely to think of Ancient Egypt, Babylonia, Greece, Rome, medieval Europe, and China. Similarly it seems probable that the second great transition will not immediately at least result in a uniform world culture but will result in a considerable variety of cultural patterns, each of them however exhibiting very similar technologies and levels of income. But it is probable that postcivilized society, simply because of the fact that its techniques are much less bound either to geography or to past culture than are the techniques of civilized society, will turn out to be much more uniform than the civilized societies have been. We see this, for instance, in the airports of the world. Air travel is a distinct mark of postcivilized society, and airports are much the same whether we find them in Bangkok or in Chicago. Similarly, steel mills are much the same in Volta Redonda in Brazil, in Birmingham, Alabama, or in India. In so far as civilization was based on agriculture, the physical basis made for wide differences. The agriculture of the Nile delta is very different from the agriculture of wheat fields of the steppes and prairies, which again is different from that of the rice paddies of Asia. We should therefore expect that civilizations based on agriculture would exhibit markedly different technological as well as cultural forms. Professor Wittfogel* has suggested indeed that the political and social institutions of civilized society are closely related to the type of agriculture from which it draws its food supply, and in particular an agriculture which requires extensive public works and irrigation like that of Ancient Egypt and China is much more likely to develop hierarchical and authoritarian societies than an agriculture based on small peasant holdings in humid lands where no public organization of any great magnitude or large public works are needed in

* Karl A. Wittfogel, *Oriental Despotism*, New Haven, Conn., Yale University Press, 1957.

order to grow food. Even in postcivilized societies, of course, rice paddies are different from wheat fields and produce a different kind of culture. Nevertheless the tractor is much the same everywhere, just as the automobile and factories are much the same everywhere, and this imposes a uniformity at least on the technological culture of the world which it never possessed before.

Furthermore the rapid and easy transportation which postcivilization permits makes it much more difficult to maintain culture traits in isolation. Civilizations could flourish at the same time on the earth which had little or no contact one with another. The Mayan civilization certainly had no contact with Rome, and Rome had very little contact with China. The transition to civilization indeed may have been accomplished in at least three independent locations or perhaps even more, though these origins are so obscure that we cannot be sure of this. Now, however, it is as easy to go halfway around the world as it used to be to go to a neighboring town, and under these circumstances an enormous process of cultural mixture is taking place which can hardly help producing much greater uniformity even in a few hundred years. It is doubtful whether a single world language will emerge in the near future, but certainly in styles of clothing, housing, mass entertainment, and transportation it is becoming increasingly hard to distinguish one part of the world from another.

An important difference which is likely to be maintained for a considerable time is that between societies which are making the transition under democratic and capitalistic institutions and those which are making the transition under institutions of totalitarian socialism. It certainly seems possible to make the technological transition under both sets of institutions. Nevertheless the societies which will emerge as a result might be quite different not only in the political and social institutions but in the value systems and the nature and quality of human life which they support. In the short run this raises many problems and unquestionably increases the danger of war and the probability that the transition will not be made. In the long perspective of history, however, this may turn out to have been a fortunate accident, if indeed it is an accident. It might well be that one of the greatest problems of postcivilized society will be how to preserve enough differentiation of human culture and how to prevent the universal spread of a drab uniformity. Cultural change and development at all times has frequently come about as a result of the interaction of cultures which previously have developed in isolation. This is a phenomenon somewhat analogous to the development of hybrid varieties in plants and animals. If we are to have hybrid cultures, however, just as if we are to have hybrid animals, there must be pure stocks maintained to interbreed. The strength of the mule and the fertility of hybrid corn would be impossible if the pure stocks from which these hybrids are derived are not maintained. Similarly in the case of cultures if we are to have vigorous hybrid cultures, the pure cultures from which these are derived must be maintained, and in a world of easy travel and rapid communication the maintenance of the pure cultures may be difficult. It may therefore be possible that things which now we regard as unfortunate sources of conflict and separation may turn out to be blessings in disguise. If socialist culture and free-market culture can develop side by side without fatal conflict, their constant interaction may be beneficial to both parties. Similarly even the development of religious sects and subcultures which are isolated from the world by what may seem a nonrational ideology may turn out to be extremely useful devices for preserving the diversity of mankind.

Perhaps the most difficult of all these problems involving diversity and uniformity is the problem of the future of different races. The different races of mankind have a sufficient sexual attraction for each other so that in the absence of any geographical or cultural obstacles to genetic mixture it is highly probable that in the course of a few thousand years the human race would become racially uniform, and the existing differences between races will be largely eliminated. From some points of view this may be very desirable, and it will certainly eliminate certain problems of interhuman conflict, most of which however are defined culturally rather than biologically. We know so little about human genetics, however, especially on the positive side of the forces which lead to genetic excellence, that it is impossible now to prophesy what may be regarded as eugenic in the future. The eugenic movement of the nineteenth century was based on inadequate knowledge of human genetics and hence could not get very far. If we develop as we may well do more accurate knowledge of the genetic factors which make for human excellence both of mind and body, the consequences for ethics, for almost all social relations, and for political behavior might be immense. But this is a bridge which we have not yet come to, and it may be well to postpone worrying about it until we do. In the meantime knowledge of human genetics, apart from a few factors making for certain defects, is not developed enough so that from it we can justify either racial purity or racial admixture. It might well be indeed that we will end by classifying mankind genetically along quite different lines from the way in which the races are now classified by strictly superficial characteristics, and we may then be able to warn against dangerous genetic combinations, as we do already with the Rh factor, and perhaps even encourage desirable combinations. Much of this, however, is in the future, though at the rate at which the biological sciences are now developing it may not be in the very distant future.

The great question as to whether the transition from civilization to postcivilization is a "good" change is one that cannot be answered completely until we know the nature and quality of different postcivilized societies. We might well argue in contemplating the first great transition from precivilized to civilized societies that in many cases this was a transition from a better state of man to a worse.

As we contemplate the innumerable wars of civilized societies, as we contemplate the hideous religion of human sacrifice and the bloody backs of innumerable slaves on which the great monuments of civilization have been built, it is sometimes hard to refrain from a certain romantic nostalgia for the "noble savage." Indeed, the *philosophes* of the eighteenth century indulged in this feeling at great length. Anthropologists have somewhat dispelled the romantic view of precivilized society, which was in many cases not only poor but cruel and disagreeable beyond even the excesses of civilization. Nevertheless it will not be difficult to contrast the best of precivilized societies and the worst of civilized societies and come out much in favor of the precivilized. Similarly a type of postcivilized society is possible as portrayed, for instance, in the anti-Utopias of George Orwell and Aldous Huxley in the middle of the twentieth century, in which the quality of human life and the dignity of man seem to be much inferior to that in the best of civilized societies.

There is clearly here a problem to be solved. We do not make men automatically good and virtuous by making them rich and powerful; indeed the truth frequently seems to be the opposite. Nevertheless we must not fall into the other trap of equating innocence with ignorance or of thinking that impotence is the same thing as virtue. An increase in power increases the potential both for good and for evil. A postcivilized society of unshakable tyranny, resting upon all the knowledge which we are going to gain in social sciences, and of unspeakable corruption resting on man's enormous power over nature, especially biological nature, is by no means inconceivable. On the other hand the techniques of postcivilization also offer us the possibility of a society in which the major sources of human misery have been eliminated, a society in which there will be no war, poverty, or disease, and in which a large majority of human beings will be able to live out their lives in relative freedom from most of the ills which now oppress a major part of mankind. This is a prize worth driving for even at the risk of tyranny and corruption. There is no real virtue in impotence, and the virtue to strive for is surely the combination of power with goodness.

In any case there is probably no way back. The growth of knowledge is one of the most irreversible forces known to mankind. It takes a catastrophe of very large dimensions to diminish the total stock of knowledge in the possession of man. Even in the rise and fall of great civilizations surprisingly little has been permanently lost, and much that was lost for a short time was easily regained. Hence there is no hope for ignorance or for a morality based on it. Once we have tasted the fruit of the tree of knowledge, as the Biblical story illustrates so well, Eden is closed to us. We cannot go back to the childhood of our race any more than we can go back to our own childhood without disaster. Eden has been lost to us forever and an angel with a flaming sword stands guard at its gates. Therefore either we must wander hopelessly in the world or we must press forward to Zion. We must learn to master ourselves as we are learning to master nature. There is no reason in the nature of things which says that ethical development is impossible, and indeed one would expect that the process of development, whether economic, political, or social, will go hand in hand with a similar process of ethical development which will enable us to use wisely the power that we have gained. This ethical development may take forms which will seem strange to us now, but just as we can trace development in the values and ethical standards of mankind as his economic and physical powers increased from precivilized society, so it is reasonable that new ethical standards will arise appropriate to the new technology of postcivilization.

We must emphasize that there is no inevitability and no determinism in making this great transition. As we shall see in subsequent chapters, there are a number of traps which lie along the way and which may either prevent man and his planet earth from making the transition altogether or delay it for many generations or even thousands of years. The first most obvious and immediate trap is the war trap. It is now theoretically possible for man to build a device which will eliminate all life from the earth. Even if this extreme event is highly improbable, less extreme disasters are at least within a range of probability that makes them a matter of serious concern. A major nuclear war would unquestionably set back the transition to a postcivilized world by many generations, and it might indeed eliminate the possibility of making this transition altogether. The effect of such war on the whole ecological system of the planet is so unpredictable that we cannot tell how large a disaster it will be, although we know it will be very large. It is possible that such a disaster will be irretrievable. It is also possible that even if we had a retrievable disaster we might not learn enough from it to retrieve ourselves. It is clear that what is desperately needed at the present time is to diminish the probability of such a disaster to the vanishing point.

Another possible trap which might delay the attainment of the transition for a long time is the population trap. This is perhaps the main reason for believing that the impact of a few postcivilized techniques on existing civilized societies might easily be disastrous in the next hundred years or so. One of the first impacts of postcivilized medicine and medical knowledge on civilized society is a large and immediate reduction in the death rate, especially in infant mortality. This is seldom if ever accompanied by a similar decrease in birth rate, and hence the first impact of postcivilized techniques on a previously stable civilized society is a tremendous upsurge in the rate of population increase. This increase may be so large that the society is incapable of adapting itself to it, and incapable in particular of devoting sufficient resources to the education of its unusually large cohorts of young people. We therefore have the tragic situation that the alleviation of much human misery and suffering in the short run may result in enormous insoluble problems in a longer period.

A third possible trap is the technological trap itself: that we may not be able to develop a genuinely stable high-level technology which is independent of exhaustible resources. Technology at the present time, even the highest technology, is largely dependent for its sources of energy and materials on accumulations in the earth which date from its geological past. In a few centuries, or at most a few thousand years, these are likely to be exhausted, and either man will fall back on a more primitive technology or he will have to advance to knowledge well beyond what he has now. Fortunately there are signs that this transition to a stable high-level technology may be accomplished, but we certainly cannot claim that it has been accomplished up to date.

A fourth possible trap may lie in the very nature of man itself. If the dangers and difficulties which now beset man are eliminated in postcivilized society and if he has no longer anything to fear but death itself, will not his creativity be diminished and may he not dissipate his energies in a vast ennui and boredom? This is a question which cannot be answered. But it lurks uneasily at the back of all optimistic statements about the long-run future of man.

All these traps will be discussed at greater length later in this book. In the meantime we may now go on to further consideration of the sources of this great transition both in the natural and the social sciences.

II.

Science as the Basis of the Great
Transition

THE great transitions in the state of mankind, both the first and the second, may be identified primarily with changes in the state of human knowledge, involving therefore a learning process. Learning is not the only source of social change. There may be profound changes, for instance, which originate in purely physical events such as the advance or retreat of ice during the Ice Age. Changes in climate, epidemics of disease, changes in the frequency of animals or the abundance of other food supplies in his environment, all may bring profound changes in man's culture. Nevertheless the long, continuous, and irreversible process which we called the great transition is concerned primarily with human learning and the processes by which knowledge is acquired. No society, no matter how primitive, whether human or animal, can exist without knowledge of some kind. The bird must know how to make a nest, the ants must know how to behave like ants. In the case of nonhuman society most of the knowledge is acquired genetically—that is, it is built into the structure of the animal by the growth processes organized by the genes. In the case of human society only a very small percentage of knowledge which is necessary to run the society, even primitive society, is acquired genetically. Almost all the human knowledge which carries on the culture has to be learned from infancy. There must therefore be resources of some kind devoted to the increase of knowledge. This we might almost call the knowledge industry, although in the primitive society this is not specialized and represents rather a certain apportionment of the time of the parents, grandparents, other relatives, and wise men of the tribe which is spent with the children and young people in teaching them the knowledge which is necessary for the culture. A good deal of this knowledge the child picks up without any formal teaching process—that is, without any time being specifically allotted by other members of the group to this end. Even in advanced societies the learning of a native language is largely done by these informal methods, and so is the learning of the many habits and customs by which people learn to communicate. In all societies, however, a certain proportion of social activity of the society must be devoted to producing, rearing, and teaching children in order to replace the skill and the knowledge which is continually lost through old age and death. From the point of view of society as a whole, knowledge is a highly depreciable commodity. Every time a man dies the knowledge which is enshrined in his organism is capital lost to the society. Even in the case of a single individual there is a constant process of forgetting and old knowledge has to be relearned.

If now the knowledge industry, or the total resources devoted to increasing knowledge in a society, is only just sufficient for replacing the knowledge which is lost through aging and death, the society will be stationary. Each generation as it grows up will replace its parents exactly in the role structure of the society. In precivilized societies, especially early ones such as the paleolithic societies, this stable condition seems to have been normal. It is hard for a modern man to conceive of a society in which children grow up to be almost exactly like their parents, generation after generation, for thousands or even hundreds of thousands of years. Our own society is so accustomed to change that it is hard for us to conceive that for the larger part of human history, at least as it extends in time, change was a great rarity and the normal condition of the society was one of stable equilibrium over long periods. Even in the midst of the advanced societies today we find little pockets of subculture, such as the Amish in the United States, who preserve their culture unchanged from generation to generation by the process of keeping their children from exposure to the world and exposing them only to the knowledge and values which are characteristic of the particular subculture.

In precivilized society, furthermore, not only is the knowledge industry so small that it barely suffices to replace the knowledge which is lost by death but innovation itself is severely frowned upon and is low in the value structure of the society. The exact reproduction of ways of the elders on the part of the young is a very high value which may not be violated without extreme penalties. This perhaps is because the margin of existence of such societies is so small that any innovation seems to threaten it, and may seem to distract attention from the essential need for transmitting the existing culture intact from one generation to the next. Where the margin of life is so precarious any innovation may seem to threaten the existence of the group, even though it may be conceived as an improvement in existing techniques.

We do not know exactly how man learned to domesticate livestock and crops and settled down to stable agriculture. We may perhaps guess from what we know of the origins of other forms of development that the advance of the ice in the last Ice Age forced paleolithic man out of his old haunts and habits and perhaps crowded him in the peninsulas of Mexico, the Mediterranean, and the Near East, where the desert makes both the coastal strip of Palestine and Syria and the Mesopotamian area virtually peninsulas. Under these circumstances overcrowding may have resulted in life getting harder as game became scarcer, with the result of increasing dissatisfaction with the old ways. It is frequently a certain worsening of the condition of a society after many generations of relative stability which first calls into question the old gods and old ways and even the wisdom of the older people. Under these circumstances there gets to be a chance for the innovator, and if an innovation is accompanied by certain charismatic phenomena the innovation may be accepted. Whatever the origins, however, we know now that the beginning of settled agriculture and the domestication of livestock were to be found about eight to ten thousand years ago in the first neolithic villages in the hill country above Mesopotamia.

Once agriculture is established the society becomes less precarious and tends to have a food surplus. Under these circumstances it may be possible to devote the surplus to an expansion of the knowledge industry, and a larger proportion as well as a much larger absolute amount of the resources of the society may be devoted to the pursuit and the transmitting of knowledge.

The first great transition actually falls into two parts which are distinct enough so that we might well speak of two transitions instead of one. The first part is the agricultural revolution, and the shift from the hunting and food-gathering cultures of the paleolithic and mesolithic to the agricultural village of the neolithic. Man still does not have metals, but he now has enough food to develop the first ideologies and missionaries, if we may so interpret the evidence of the megalithic monuments that stretch from the Mediterranean to Carnac in Brittany and Stonehenge in Britain. From its origins in the Near East the agricultural revolution spread west to the Atlantic and east to China, and perhaps even east to America, though it is still problematic whether the neolithic agriculture and civilizations of Mexico and Peru are spontaneous innovations or imitations carried by early "missionaries" across the Bering Strait. Then about 3000 B.C. comes the second part of the first great transition, the urban revolution; the food surplus from agriculture is now gathered into cities; metallurgy begins, as agriculture began, in the mountains north of Mesopotamia. The first cities arise in Mesopotamia, and the industrial revolution based on metals, plays an important role in this development.

From the point of view of long-run developments, however, the invention of writing is even more important than the invention of smelting and metalworking. Furthermore, writing goes along with schools, which are found in the ruins of the earliest cities. This gives us a new instrument for cultural transmission.

Again we know very little about the origins of the innovation. But we know that it is almost contemporaneous with the development of the first cities and civilization itself. Just as the development of agriculture permitted a larger proportion of resources of a society to be devoted to the knowledge industry, so writing represents a tremendous technological improvement in the knowledge industry. For the first time in the story of mankind the knowledge of a society did not depend merely on verbal transmission and on being contained in the minds of the old men. It could be written down so that the past could speak to the present, and the knowledge of the society could be preserved even though the heads which once contained it were dead and gone. Preliterate society is always in terrible danger of a devastating loss of knowledge through death. If, for instance, an epidemic kills off the old men before they have transmitted the traditions of the tribe to the young, the knowledge is irrevocably lost. With the invention of writing, knowledge can be preserved on tablets or papyrus, and even if the scribes or the wise men who hold the knowledge in their heads die, as long as the writing can be read the knowledge can be relearned by the young. Writing furthermore can be copied, and this means that books can be written and knowledge spread among the population in a more efficient way than the face-to-face contact which was necessary before. In a preliterate society, knowledge can be passed on only from its possessor to a very small group who can sit around him and listen to his words. In a literate society, knowledge can be passed on to a large number of people at the same time through the agency of books even when these have to be made laboriously by hand. A book once made can be read many times, by many people, for many years.

Once a society has written records not only is the danger of loss of knowledge much diminished but knowledge is almost bound to accumulate. The present is always able to add to the store of knowledge received from the past, even though in the early days some written knowledge was lost in catastrophes such as the fall of the Cretan Empire, the burning of the library of Alexandria, or the "burning of the books" in China. The danger of loss is much less than in a preliterate society, and a very much larger quantity of knowledge can be stored in books or in a library than can possibly be stored in a single head or even a group of heads. A literate civilized society therefore cannot be static as a precivilized society can be. The very existence of writing prevents this because there is a constant accumulation of knowledge and as knowledge accumulates the society is bound to change. The first civilized societies were very small and contained to our minds astonishingly small numbers of people. Many of these societies were overthrown by war, and the knowledge which they contained apparently was lost. Nevertheless throughout the whole period of civilization one suspects that there has been an almost constant although slow accumulation of knowledge and that the accumulation always outweighed the loss except in periods of extreme violence and decay. On the other hand it must be pointed out that a good deal of knowledge which is characteristic of civilized societies is ceremonial knowledge which is useless from the point of view of economic development or technical change narrowly conceived. A good deal of the knowledge is false knowledge—that is, it consists of propositions which are not true and may actually be a negative factor in human welfare; for instance, the so-called knowledge which the Aztecs believed they possessed that without a large amount of human sacrifices the corn will not grow must be regarded as a liability rather than an asset to the society. All civilized societies are heavily weighed down with superstition, and indeed the instability of all civilized societies and the fact that each one rarely lasted for more than a few hundred years is evidence of the fact that the base of the knowledge on which they were founded was inadequate and frequently harmful.

Even in civilized societies the bulk of knowledge which is acquired is what might be called folk knowledge, in the sense that it is acquired either in the family or in the face-to-face group rather than in formal education or in schools. It is highly characteristic of civilized societies that they are divided sharply into two classes: those who possess school knowledge, which is transmitted in books and libraries and by professional teachers, and those who possess only the folk knowledge. The former, of course, are the elite and the rulers, and the latter are the mass of peasants and ordinary people who are the ruled. The folk knowledge accumulates very slowly if at all, mainly because it is associated so deeply with the parent-child relationship that any questioning of it is a questioning of the authority of parents. In a folk culture this authority is so strong that any questioning of it is associated immediately with a betrayal of the deepest values of the group. A harmful superstition therefore perpetuates itself generation after generation, because the superstitions are hard to test, and furthermore it would be considered impious to test them. Many of the difficulties in initiating a process of economic development in traditional and merely civilized societies today is that this process always involves a certain undermining of the authority of the parents, especially of the mother, and hence can lead to psychological difficulties.

In all civilized societies the ruling class has schools and has a certain amount of formal education outside the family. Even here, however, change in the body of knowledge which is taught is often difficult. The knowledge is frequently enshrined in sacred books whose authority is not to be questioned and which indeed become a kind of parent substitute. A great emphasis is placed in the schools on learning the classics whether these are the Chinese classics, the Bible, the Koran, or the work of Aristotle. Under these circumstances even the schools of the ruling class do not differ much in the nature of the transmission of their knowledge from the folk knowledge of the poor. It is therefore no wonder that in spite of the great advantage which literacy and the rise of books give to the accumulation of knowledge, in a society of classical civilization the increase of knowledge is extremely slow and indeed the innovator is still often regarded with great suspicion. But however much the society puts the brakes on the accumulation of knowledge it never seems to be able to prevent this accumulation altogether. From ancient Sumeria up to the

European Middle Ages, to nineteenth-century Japan and twentieth-century India and China a continuous growth of civilized knowledge can be traced.

Just as agriculture paved the way for the development of writing and civilization, so the slow growth of knowledge in the course of civilization paves the way for the second great transition and the rise of science. The origins of this movement are less obscure than the origins of the first transition. Nevertheless there are many puzzling problems involved in tracing them, in spite of the fact that a pretty continuous growth of knowledge and improvement in technology can be traced, especially in Western Europe, from about the sixth century A.D. It is reasonable to assign a crucial place to the invention of printing in the fifteenth century in Europe. It is an interesting question why the invention of printing in China, which took place even earlier, did not produce a like revolution there, but it may be that the difficult nature of Chinese language prevented printing from having the kind of impact which it had in Europe. Like the invention of writing itself the invention of printing must be regarded as another technological improvement in the knowledge industry, particularly in the dissemination of knowledge.

Another prescientific invention which, like printing, laid the foundation for the rise of science was clockwork. The fifteenth century in Europe witnessed some remarkable advances in mechanical engineering, especially in the development of clockwork mechanisms of great ingenuity and complexity of design. Unquestionably these successes turned men's minds generation after generation toward mechanical explanations of the universe rather than animistic ones. In the sixteenth century the Reformation shocked the established intellectual order, and even though intellectually it may not have represented a very radical break with the past, by creating new ideals and breaking up the monolithic system of the Middle Ages it at least removed some of the obstacles to the development of new ideas. The strength of any authority depends a good deal on its never being challenged. If it is once challenged successfully in one sphere, there is much greater probability of its being challenged in another. If Luther could successfully challenge the spiritual and temporal authority of the Pope, then others might hope to be able to challenge the authority of Aristotle or Galen. The road that leads to science might well be compared to a maze. In some societies, for instance in China, many promising beginnings seem to have led to dead ends. In Europe, perhaps more by good luck than good management, in spite of the many dead ends that were explored, there always seemed to be somebody who could find the open path, even though the path that led to Newton and Einstein was a tortuous one.

The rise of science might be described as a mutation in scholarship. We have already noticed the tremendous importance of writing in that it permitted the development of a literate subculture extending through time. Folk cultures by and large are cultures of the here and now. They may have the memories of heroes and some stories from the past, but by and large they are concerned overwhelmingly with the present. With the development of writing we get the subculture of scholarship in which books created by minds long dead can have as powerful an influence as the words of the living. The scholar lives and moves within a network of communication that extends many centuries into the past. In this sense a scientist is also a scholar, but he is something more. Whereas a scholar is mainly concerned with detailed study of the texts which come down from the past and is concerned mainly with the form of the written word, the scientist is concerned with reading the book of nature as well as the works of man. This image indeed was frequently used as a justification in the earlier days of science. Furthermore just as a scholar pores over the works of the past and studies them word by word, so the scientist pores over the book of nature with extremely careful observation. By this means a new way of organizing the growth of knowledge on a more rapid and more secure basis than had been known before slowly developed. It begins with isolated individuals in the fifteenth and sixteenth centuries. By the seventeenth century scientists have become a small international community bound together by an active correspondence and publication, and they are beginning to organize into societies. The foundation of the Royal Society in London in the latter half of the seventeenth century is a crucial date. Here science begins to emerge as an organized subculture. Even then science was still largely a work of amateurs, and the amateur period of science lasted well into the nineteenth century. It is only in the twentieth century that science has become a substantial, organized part of society on a full-time professional basis.

We must now go on to examine the nature of this revolution in the knowledge industry in more detail. The process of the growth of knowledge involves three concepts: the image, the inference or expectation which is derived from it, and the message which either confirms it or denies it. The image is the actual content of a particular human mind—that is, it is the subjective content of knowledge.* This is what a man thinks the world is like, the sum total of his beliefs, his image of the world and himself and space and time, his ideas of causal connections, and so on. From our image of the world we constantly draw inferences about the future—that is, we derive expectations of what is going to happen. I have an expectation, for instance, that tomorrow morning I shall travel from my house to a certain room and shall begin to lecture to a class which I shall find assembled there. This expectation is drawn from my image of space, time, and causality, from my image of the social system in which I believe I am placed, and so on.

Our image is subject to a constant input of messages from our immediate environment. These messages may

* For a further exposition of this concept, see K. E. Boulding, *The Image,* University of Michigan Press, 1956.

either confirm our expectations or disappoint them. I may go into class tomorrow morning and find nobody in the room. Messages from my eyes and ears which I expected do not arrive. Under the pressure of disappointment something is bound to happen. I can in fact do one of three things. I can deny the truth of the messages and say that it was a false message or illusion. I can deny the truth of the inference which gave rise to the expectation, and say that I should not have expected the messages which failed to come. The third possibility is that I may change the image itself. Thus if I go to class tomorrow and find nobody there I may say to myself that I am dreaming and that the message was a false one, and I try to wake up. If I am convinced that I am awake and that my senses do not deceive me and that the messages cannot be denied, then I may deny the inference. I may decide that I thought it was Thursday when in fact it was Wednesday, when I do not have a class, or I may decide it was a public holiday of which I was not aware. My basic image here remains unchanged but I have reorganized the inference which I have drawn from it. If, however, I can neither reject the message nor reject the inference, there is no course open to me but to reorganize my image of the world. I may decide that I have been fired or suspended or that in any case I am not what I thought and the social system in which I am placed has radically changed.

The mentally ill, especially the schizophrenics and the paranoids, are incapable of reorganizing their images of the world because such reorganization would be too painful to them. They therefore either reject messages or inferences constantly in the face of disappointment of expectations. The paranoid, for instance, may be convinced that everybody hates him, and he interprets every action on the part of others as confirming his belief. A friendly gesture is always interpreted as having a sinister motive. In extreme cases of schizophrenia the schizophrenic obtains complete control of his sense data. Hence he actually sees, hears, and touches the things that he imagines, and no aspect of the real world can come through to him. Everything comes from his image, so nothing can shake it.

While it is obvious that the complete rigidity in the image prevents the growth of knowledge altogether, it is by no means clear what are the conditions under which the growth of a true image of the world proceeds most rapidly. We have here a system with too many degrees of freedom for comfort. Even though complete rigidity in the image prevents any increase in knowledge, complete flexibility may be equally disastrous. Sometimes the inferences that we have drawn are wrong and sometimes the messages that we receive are defective. Under these circumstances a certain rigidity in the image is desirable. We do not believe, for instance, that the stick is actually bent when it is placed in water, and we do not believe that objects are continually changing in size as they seem to do when they approach us or recede from us.

In social systems the case is even clearer. The inferences are often very hard to draw and messages are frequently ambiguous. If something we read in a newspaper contradicts our image of the world, it is at least not an absurd assumption that what we read in a newspaper was wrong or was deliberately intended to mislead us. Furthermore in systems in which the inferences are only probable—and almost all social systems are of this nature—disappointment of expectations may simply be due to bad luck, and we have to have a large number of observations before we can learn much about the nature of the probability. Furthermore all our messages pass through a filter or censor, and messages which support an existing image are much more likely to get through this filter than messages which are contradictory to our image. This is particularly likely to be the case where the nature of our image of the world is closely bound up with our identity in our own eyes and in the value which we place on our own person. A man, for instance, who has built his whole life and identity around a particular ideology will be most unwilling to change the image of the world which his ideology implies, for he seemingly cannot change his image without denying his own identity as a person. Under these circumstances his system of values itself creates a filter which is likely to filter out all the messages which are contradictory to his image of his own identity. Occasionally of course there are conversions—that is, a person rejects the former image and identity that went with it and reorganizes this person into a new identity around a new image. These, however, are rare, especially in later life.

The persistence of superstition even into a supposedly scientific age is testimony to the power of traditional images in ambiguous situations. It is a curious fact, for instance, that even in the most advanced societies the daily paper frequently carries a column of astrological advice in spite of the fact that astrology has long been exposed as a pseudo science. It persists, however, because its predictions are ambiguous enough so that it is relatively easy to fit the messages we receive into the plastic expectations it creates, and presumably the predictions give some people a sense of security about the future in what seems to them a dangerous and uncertain world.

How then did the scientific subculture as it developed from the seventeenth century on manage to produce an image of the world with a continually increasing reality, at least as judged by the power over nature which it seems to have given to its fortunate possessors? The answer may be found along a number of lines. In the first place the scientific images of the world were on the whole concerned with the aspects of reality which did not involve deeply the identity of the people holding them. This is not altogether true. Galileo had considerable difficulty, we may recall, in reconciling his identity as a scientist with his identity as a Catholic. Even in the twentieth century scientists in the Soviet Union have experienced some difficulty in reconciling their identity as scientists with their identity as Russians or Communists, especially in the field of biology. For reasons which are still not entirely clear, however, the scientific community in the course of its development created an ethic and standard of value in which the truth took precedence over any individual identity, however deeply cherished. In the scientific ethic the scientist is supposed to be delighted if his own theory is proved wrong. In practice this delight is often moderate. Scientists are human, and the identity of a man is more closely bound than we are supposed to think with the particular theories which he has developed or espoused. There have been many cases in the history of science of bitter personal controversies in which the unwillingness of the scientist to sacrifice theories around which he built his own identity was a real handicap to the advancement of knowledge. Nevertheless these cases are the exceptions rather than the rule, and a considerable part of the success of the scientific community in advancing knowledge must be attributed to its value system in which an impersonal devotion to truth is regarded as the highest value to which both personal and national pride must be subordinated.

The second major reason for the success of the scientific community is that it protected itself against the rejection of its inferences or rejection of its messages or observations. If observations fail to confirm a theoretical image, the scientific community has protected itself against a failure of inference by the extended use of mathematics in its theoretical models and in the expectations which are derived from them. This meant that there was a necessity about the inferences which a purely empirical system of inferences does not possess. The inferences of science are drawn not from observation but from theories. This is a crucial point which is often imperfectly understood. Thus we have observed that the sun has risen many times in the past and hence we infer by a simple projection of past experience that the sun will rise tomorrow. This is not a scientific inference but an empirical one, and in complex systems it can easily be fallacious. A couple, for instance, who seem to have been happily married for twenty-five years may suddenly get divorced. Countries which have been enemies for centuries may suddenly become reconciled. A dog which has been gentle for years may suddenly bite his master. By contrast the scientific inference is derived from the logic of the system itself. Thus the motion of the planets is derived from the law of inverse squares by a logical or mathematical necessity. Scientific inference therefore always takes the form of conditional inference. "If A is true, then B is true." This says nothing about whether A or B is in fact true. It merely establishes a necessary relationship between them.

It is not impossible even for scientists to fall into logical error. Logical error, however, has this extraordinary property that once it is found out it is extraordinarily hard to repeat it. Logic, that is to say, is a social system in which an error always has a finite expectation of life. There are high rewards furthermore for the detection of error, and it is therefore very rare for logical error to go undetected for long.

It is more difficult to protect oneself against error in the messages or observation than against error in logic. The progress of science in this regard has largely been the result of a remarkable series of inventions directed toward increasing the range and the sensitivity of man's message-receiving apparatus. It is no accident that the great advance of science began with the invention of the telescope and the microscope, both of which represent as it were extensions of human eyes, one in the direction of perceiving things which are large and distant and the other in the direction of perceiving things which are small and near. The process in the extension of man's senses continues today with the electronic microscope and radio astronomy. It also continues into the social sciences with the development of statistical techniques for the indexing and processing of large quantities of information and also with the development of sampling surveys which extend the range of human observation from man's immediate social surroundings to society at large. The more refined the methods of observation the more refined can be the theoretical systems and the inferences which are drawn from them.

The method of science then may be summarized very briefly by saying that in the scientific subculture, expectations are deliberately created by necessary inferences from theoretical models, within the range of observations suitable to the delicacy of the enlarged apparatus of the human senses. If these expectations are disappointed then the images or models on which they are based must be reorganized, as there is no possibility of denying the inference and very little possibility of denying the messages which do not conform to the expectations. The classic example of this process is perhaps the Michelson-Morley experiment on the velocity of light. According to the older Newtonian image of space and time, the fact that the earth has an apparent velocity through space demanded the inference that the velocity of light would be different in different directions. The experiment showed that this was not so and forced a radical reorganization of the scientific image of space and time which produced the theory of relativity.

The essential difference between scientific images and folk or prescientific images may be illustrated by the example of rain control. Many primitive peoples have believed that rain dances produce rain. This belief furthermore is deeply built into the identity of the tribe, and anyone who questions it in effect denies the whole being of the tribe and is apt to be driven from it, or else he just keeps quiet. This is an empirical, not a logical inference. There is no mathematical or logical system by which we can demonstrate any necessary connection between rain dances and rain. Whatever logic there is is by analogy: some such argument as, "The gods produce rain if they are pleased. Men are pleased by dances, therefore the gods will be pleased by dances. Therefore dances produce rain." The image that rain dances produce rain is a stable one, not only because to question it would be to question the identity of the tribe but also because there is virtually no way of disproving a purely empirical inference. The proposition is that a rain dance causes rain. If the rain dance is performed and it rains, this of course confirms the proposition. Unfortunately if a rain dance is performed and it does not rain, this also confirms the proposition. Rain dances are complicated and easy to do wrong. Therefore, if a rain dance is done and rain does not follow, there can always be a profitable heart searching in which it will invariably be discovered that something was wrong with the rain dance. Therefore the proposition that a rain dance properly performed produces rain remains unscathed.

By contrast let us look at the scientific method of producing rain by means of cloud seeding. In point of fact this is probably not much more successful than rain dances. Nevertheless it is based on an extraordinarily different process of the growth of knowledge. Observation on the spot with sensitive instruments has revealed that clouds consist of small drops of water and that if these drops are big enough it will rain. It can be shown mathematically that under certain conditions there is a relation between the size of a nucleus and the formation of these drops. It is therefore inferred that if a very fine dust, for instance of silver iodide, is thrown into a cloud from an airplane, this will cause drops to condense, which otherwise would not have happened, and rain will fall. Unfortunately the atmosphere is an enormously complicated system with many other variables in it, and these other variables frequently upset the prediction. The prediction, however, is based on a logical inference, not on an empirical inference. And to this extent it has the promise that as more and more observations are made, as the better theories are developed, and as the system of the atmostphere is better understood we will have a better chance of being able to control it. Whereas the folk image is by its very nature static, the scientific image is constantly subject to revision in the light of deliberately acquired information and deliberately provoked disappointments.

It remains to point out the relation between the development of science on the one hand and the development of technology on the other. Economic development consists essentially in the improvement of what Adam Smith called the "productive powers of labor." It means simply that man can produce more with an hour of his activity than he could before. Interestingly enough, Adam Smith as early as 1776 had identified the main causes of the improvement in the productive powers of labor as related to the growth of knowledge. He lists three main causes. The first is the increase in dexterity and skill which comes with the division of labor and the fact that man applies himself continuously to a particular craft. This is essentially a learning process at the level of the lower nervous system. A craftsman learns his skill by trial and error and repeated practice in very much the same way the baby learns to walk. Adam Smith's second cause for economic development is of minor importance. It is that as people become specialized to a particular occupation they save the time which is commonly lost in going from one occupation to another. This is also an economy in the learning process. It takes us a little while even when we are renewing an old occupation to "warm up" and to relearn the old skill. Adam Smith's third cause is by far the most important one. It is "the invention of the great number of machines which facilitate and abridge labor and enable one man to do the work of many." Adam Smith says, however, that the development of machines takes place through three different kinds of processes. First, there may be improvement by the workmen who actually operate the machine. Second, there may be improvements by the specialized maker of machines, each one anxious to improve his competitive position in the field by making a better machine. The third cause, however, in the long run is the most important of all, and is what we would now call research and development. It is worth quoting at length. "All the improvements in machinery, however, have by no means been the inventions of those who had occasion to use the machines. Many improvements have been made by the ingenuity of the makers of the machines, when to make them became the business of a peculiar trade; and some by that of those who are called philosophers or men of speculation, whose trade it is not to do any thing, but to observe everything, and who, upon that account, are often capable of combining together the powers of the most distant and dissimilar objects. In the progress of society, philosophy or

speculation becomes, like every other employment, the principal or sole trade and occupation of a particular class of
citizens. Like every other employment too, it is subdivided
into a great number of different branches, each of which
affords occupation to a particular tribe or class of philosophers; and this subdivision at employment in philosophy,
as well as in every other business, improves dexterity and
saves time. Each individual becomes more expert in his
own peculiar branch, more work is done upon the whole,
and the quantity of science is considerably increased by it."*

This extraordinary farseeing passage foreshadows a development which was still of minor importance in Adam
Smith's own day: the growth of organized applied research
in the development of useful knowledge and improved
methods of production. Before, the advance of science improvements in production were largely a matter of folk
knowledge, discovered by unconscious skill, accident, or
happy observation, and passed on largely by the face-to-
face contact between the master of a craft and his ap-
prentices. Improvement, even though it is slow, is almost
always in the positive direction, with local reversals. Before
the age of science, however, it took man an inconceivably
long time to think up what seem to us obvious mechanical
devices or objects such as the stirrup or the crank. Even
when they are invented, the diffusion of improved methods
is often quite slow. The scientific image of the world gives

* Adam Smith, *An Inquiry into the Nature and Causes of the
Wealth of Nations*, Book 1, Chapter I.

us methods of technology which could not possibly have been achieved in the past. The ancients could never have produced a dynamo, or made aluminum, or released nuclear energy, or for that matter made a practicable airplane or internal combustion engine.

Furthermore the technology which is based on science participates in the rapid growth of science itself. It is hard to think of any advance in pure science which has not opened the door to a new advance in technology. An astonishingly large proportion of people in the advanced countries today are engaged in the production of goods and services which were totally unknown to their grandfathers. It may indeed be that this process will eventually move toward an end, and man's knowledge of the universe and therefore his technology will eventually be stabilized. That day, however, seems a very long way off. We have not even adapted ourself to the nuclear revolution, and already the spectacular advance in the present generation in the biological sciences promises an even more spectacular and alarming expansion of man's powers. And on the heels of the biological sciences come the social sciences. Already social science has challenged the folk images of man and society in a way that is profoundly disturbing to old and settled ways. This, however, is the subject of the next chapter.

III.

The Significance of the Social Sciences

THE scientific revolution has not been confined to man's image of the physical or biological world. It has likewise extended into his image of himself and of the society which he created and in which he as an individual is embedded. This is the field of social science, which ordinarily embraces economics, psychology, sociology, political science, and anthropology. Certain aspects of geography, history, and linguistics should be included in this list. Geography in a sense studies all sciences in so far as they are related to distribution on the surface of the earth, and human geography is an important element in the social sciences. History has a somewhat ambiguous status. In one sense it provides the raw material for all the sciences, for the record of the past is the only raw material we have. The historian, however, perhaps because he deals with the social system as a whole as it stands in time and space, is also unwilling to develop theoretical models because of the very complexity of the system with which he deals. The problem of the testing of theoretical systems is usually difficult in history, and it is therefore not surprising to find that the historian frequently occupies an uneasy position between the social scientist on the one hand and the pure literary humanist on the other. Literary and linguistic studies likewise straddle the boundary between the humanities and the social sciences.

By comparison with the physical and even biological sciences the social sciences often seem immature. They cannot claim any practical success as spectacular as the release of nuclear energy or the elimination of a disease. This immaturity is sometimes explained as the effect of youth. The social sciences, however, are not so young as they are sometimes supposed to be. The crucial date in the birth of science is the point in time at which its fundamental theoretical structure is first formulated; a theoretical structure which is then capable of successive refinement and modification in the light of further evidence. For physics this crucial date is unquestionably the appearance of Newton's *Principia* in the late seventeenth century. Economics may well claim to be the next oldest science, for its critical stage is reached with Adam Smith in 1776. In *The Wealth of Nations* we have all the essential elements of a theoretical system, and in a sense everything that has happened in economics since has been refinement of the fundamental system laid down by Adam Smith. Chemistry is the next oldest science. Its fundamental theoretical formulation has been made by Dalton in the early part of the nineteenth century. Darwin in the mid-nineteenth century represents the similar point in the development of biological science. It is harder to put similar dates on the other social sciences, as the theoretical formulation has emerged more slowly and is not associated with any dramatic personal achievements. By the early part of the twentieth century, however, it is reasonable to claim that sociology, psychology, and anthropology either have been born as sciences or were close to it. Political science has been the most backward of all the sciences and is only now beginning to approach a genuinely scientific formulation.

One of the most important aspects of the scientific revolution in general is the continuous conflict between the folk images of the world, which are built up out of the ordinary experience of man and from the generalization of this experience, and the scientific images which arise out of the organized expansion of knowledge. The fundamental difference between scientific knowledge and folk knowledge, as we saw in the previous chapter, is that the folk knowledge is derived essentially from empirical inference and casual observation where as scientific knowledge is derived from necessary inference from theoretical models according to the mathematical logic and carefully organized observation guided by inventions which extend the power of the senses. Scientific and folk images are frequently inconsistent, and as it is always painful to abandon an image, a struggle between the two ensues. The superior power of scientific images usually ensures the triumph of the scientific image over the competing folk image, but nevertheless the struggle may be long and painful.

The seventeenth and eighteenth centuries, for instance, saw the triumph of the Copernican and the Newtonian views of the universe as against both the simple folk image of the flat earth with the sun and the heavenly bodies pursuing their courses across the dome of the sky, and the more sophisticated but still inadequate "scientific" image of the earth-centered Ptolemaic universe. But this triumph was not accomplished without cost. In the folk image of space and time, man is at the center of a very cozy little universe which surrounds him. In the scientific image, man is an occupant of a minute planet revolving around a minor sun in an insignificant and remote arm of a commonplace galaxy in a billion-galaxied universe. This change may be deeply disturbing to man's self-respect unless it goes along with a certain shift in his values toward a deeper humility than he has usually achieved. Similarly in the nineteenth century the evolutionary view of the history of life and of the universe led to an enormous expansion of man's image of the time scale, by contrast with the folk image of special creation and a history of only six thousand years. There has likewise been a long struggle between scientific and folk images within the medical profession, and it is only within the last two hundred years that medicine has emerged as a scientific discipline capable of curing more disease than it created.

In the twentieth century we now face a similar struggle

between the folk images of man himself and of his society as against the more sophisticated images which are being created by the social sciences. I do not want to imply, especially at this point, that scientific images are always true and folk images always false. In the course of history, science has produced many false images, and there are strong folk elements in many points of view which claim the name of science, especially in the social sciences. Furthermore man is an enormously complicated piece of organization and his societies are even more complicated. Man arrives at knowledge about himself partly by outside observation and partly by inner reflection and self-examination. The scientific method is much easier to apply to external observation than it is to internal observation. It is therefore not surprising that the social sciences have tended to neglect the knowledge which was derived from internal observation and have frequently left this aspect of man's knowledge of himself to the poets, the dramatists, and the humanists.

There is a certain fundamental distinction between man's knowledge of himself and of his own society and his knowledge of the nonhuman universe. In the case of the nonhuman world our only source of knowledge is external observation. The physicist has never been an electron, the biologist has never been a cell. By contrast the psychologist is a man and the sociologist has been a member of a family and even the economist has occasionally spent money. In the study of himself, therefore, man has both an "inside track" and an "outside track." The inside track is derived from the fact that he is himself an example of the system which he studies. Hence he has inside knowledge of it in a way that he has not of external systems. The outside track is that he is able to study himself as an object outside of himself. The outside track is frequently associated with scientific knowledge and the inside with folk or humanistic knowledge. The social scientist is frequently inclined to deprecate the inside track and to pretend that he operates only on the outside track. If we examine the social scientists carefully, however, we shall find that in all cases they do in fact rely in part on inside knowledge and internal observation, and their theoretical models owe a great deal to the power of man to know himself from the inside.

Unlike the situation in, say, astronomy, the conflict between scientific images and folk images in the social sciences is not a wholly unequal conflict, and is not necessarily resolved by a clear victory of one side or the other. Rather, we may expect a certain accommodation and even mutual assistance in the two sides of a man's search for knowledge of himself. Psychology does not destroy the insights of Shakespeare into human nature though it may illuminate these insights and reinforce them. We should expect literature to be ultimately enriched by the knowledge which is derived from the social sciences. Similarly the wise social scientists will not neglect the rich insights which are derived from the poets, and will use these in the formulation of theoretical models.

Freud is a good example of a man who combined in a

creative way the poetical or humanistic insight with the careful observation techniques of the sciences. In man's images of himself indeed the Freudian revolution has produced a fundamental shift which is almost of the order of magnitude of the Copernican revolution in his images of space. This is in spite of, or perhaps because of, the fact that the Freudian system is not pure science but has strong elements of folk and humanistic knowledge in it. The very fact, for instance, that its terminology is largely drawn from the classical Greek drama is evidence of its debt to poetic insight. It is, however, a system which is within the scientific domain in so far as it is subject to testing. In the light of the complexity of the system, this testing is extremely difficult. Nevertheless we may expect the system to be modified and even some aspects of it radically changed in the light of further organized experience. It is clear, for instance, that many of the Freudian theoretical formulations are of limited applicability because they are derived essentially from the peculiar subculture of bourgeois Vienna of the late nineteenth century, and it is recognized that different cultures produce different kinds of disorder. Nevertheless the basic concept of the unconscious and the even more basic concept that a person's present condition is the result of his total experience up to the present remain in all cultures. And as evidence accumulates we gain more accurate knowledge of the particular relationships in each culture between, say, childhood experiences and adult behavior.

In economics, likewise, we find the development of scientific and theoretical images of the economic system from Adam Smith to the present day. This image in many respects is very different from the folk image of what the economic system is like. The folk image of the economy is derived by generalization from personal experience. The economist by contrast has the image of the economic system as a whole, exhibiting properties which are not found in the individual experience. Thus to the individual, expenditure and receipts are very different things, and he may allow one to exceed the other without any difficulty. From the point of view of a closed economic system as a whole, expenditure and receipts are exactly the same thing, simply because every expenditure is a receipt for someone else and every receipt is an expenditure from someone else. For closed economic systems it is therefore impossible for total receipts and total expenditures to be different. An individual similarly sees debt from his own point of view as a pure liability. An economist sees that every liability is an asset for someone else, and hence he has a very different attitude toward debt, especially the national debt. There is therefore a conflict between the technical point of view of the economist and the unsophisticated point of view of the untrained person. Conflicts of this kind develop in socialist economies just as they do in market economies. The trained economist in the socialist society realizes, for instance, that the price system—and even the interest rate—has a fundamental economic function. The ordinary party member and commissar, and often even the main decision makers, regard the price system as a kind of enemy to be beaten down, and they make many disastrous mistakes in policy as a result.

The findings of social psychology have already begun to affect the structure and conduct of organizations both in business and in government. The whole atmosphere of industrial relations in the advanced countries has been profoundly changed by the application of certain principles first developed in the social sciences. The findings of anthropology have had a profound effect on the whole institution of colonialism and also on the missionary enterprise. These changes do not occur without strain, and where the strain is too great there is real danger of an anti-intellectual or antiscientific reaction on the part of the outraged "folk." The wisdom that is handed down from our parents is something precious to us, and if it is challenged too sharply we may, as it were, rush to their defense and attempt to deny or overthrow the intruding ideas. The antievolution laws of Tennessee and the Scopes Trial which resulted is a good example of this kind of reaction. In the struggle of the scientific image against the folk image, however, in the natural and biological sciences, the scientific image has everywhere been victorious, simply because of its obviously greater power.

In the case of the social sciences, as we have seen, the struggle is more complex, because of the fact that there are many quasi-scientific images which develop a following and a folk loyalty. Marxism, Freudian analysis, Jungian psychology, Rudolf Steiner's anthroposophy, Galton's eugenics, all represent premature crystallizations of social science which became imbued with certain "folk" loyalties. All these various doctrines owe a good deal to the rising body of social-science knowledge, and without this they never would have developed. The moment, however, that a body of ideas attaches to itself the loyalty of a group of followers and becomes, in a sense, a dogma, it ceases thereby to be part of the continuing and expanding body of scientific knowledge. In the social sciences, therefore, we struggle not only against ordinary folk knowledge but against what might be called folk science. In spite of this a body of genuinely testable knowledge about man and society does seem to grow, and we may have even greater expectations of its growth for the future.

Even a relatively imperfect shift from the folk image of man and society to a scientific image involves man in at least two large, irreversible, and related changes. The first of these is the increase in self-consciousness, not only of the individual himself but also of the society in which he has been placed. Individual self-consciousness almost certainly develops as early as spoken language, and it is the major characteristic which distinguishes man from all his predecessors. The fact that totemism is perhaps the first body of theoretical ideas evolved by the human race suggests that the self-consciousness of early man was deeply bound up with his perception of himself as both different from and akin to the animals. Self-consciousness, however, is a mysterious process about which we know very little. Up to now, at any rate, we do not have the slightest idea of how to make a self-conscious machine, which indicates how very far we are from objective scientific knowledge in this area.

Social self-consciousness comes very much later than personal self-consciousness in man's development. A primitive man or even a civilized man largely accepts the society in which he grows up without any self-consciousness of it. Everything about it seems perfectly natural to him and he never questions it. Even when he becomes conscious of other societies outside his own, he is apt to dismiss these as inferior or strange, for the ways of his fathers seem to be the only right and natural ways of conducting a society. Even in quite advanced societies this attitude is very common. The Chinese regarded themselves as the Middle Kingdom and the natural center of world culture. The Greeks regarded the non-Greeks as barbarians. The English and Americans not very long ago regarded with supreme self-confidence their own societies as having the right and natural way of doing everything, and regarded everybody else as inferior or peculiar. With the development of social self-consciousness, man, as it were, steps outside his own social skin and looks at himself and at his own society from the outside.

In this process the social sciences play an extremely important role, because it is part of the myth of the social scientist that he stands outside his own society in observing it. It may be possible for social self-consciousness to arise even in a folk culture if people have many contacts with other cultures outside them which they regard as valid as their own even though different. But this is very rare, and it is at least plausible to suppose that a genuine social self-consciousness only arises with the rise of a social-scientific point of view. There is a certain analogy here to the Copernican revolution. Before Copernicus, man looked at the universe, as it were, from his own point of view, with the earth as the center. Similarly, before the advent of social self-consciousness every man looks at the world as if his own society were the center of it. The development of a scientific point of view, whether in astronomy or the social sciences, destroys this homocentric attitude, and just as man now sees himself as an inhabitant of a rather obscure planet, no more at the center of the universe, so he sees his own society as a cultural planet in a world of planets rather than as a sun, and as one among many of the possible ways of ordering human life and relations.

I was once with a group of academic people on the Fourth of July, in a university town in the middle of the United States, when the fireworks were beginning in the city park. One of the group—an American anthropologist —said to the rest of us, "Let's go and see the tribal rites," and we all went off to enjoy the patriotic occasion. The remark has profound implications of social self-consciousness. First of all, the speaker identified the occasion as a special case of a large class of social events, and by so doing, he in effect separated himself from the event and stood outside it. His less sophisticated ancestors and even many of his contemporaries would not have had any feeling that these celebrations were "tribal rites," and they would simply have regarded the occasion as the right and proper thing to do on the Fourth of July without ever questioning the matter.

There are disadvantages as well as advantages in social self-consciousness of this kind. It is by no means an unmixed blessing. It may be fine for philosophers "not to do anything, but to observe everything," but if everybody is a philosopher not very much will be done. In an age of social science and universal education, however, everyone in a sense becomes a philosopher. The detachment which this engenders may lead to a certain unwillingness to perform the humdrum tasks or to take the necessary risks which are involved in the conduct of society itself. But this is a problem which must be mastered along with self-consciousness, both at the personal and at the social level, for once self-consciousness is acquired, there is virtually no way of losing it. The fact that self-consciousness can become pathological, as in the case of a person getting stage fright, does not mean that the pathological element cannot be controlled. There may be an equivalent of stage fright in the self-consciousness of society. Indeed one sometimes thinks the United States is suffering from it at the moment. But again there is no way back to naïveté; we have to go forward to a healthy self-consciousness by curing its pathological states.

A second characteristic of the shift from the folk image to the scientific image of society is the development of what might be called the systems point of view. This is very closely related to social self-consciousness and is in considerable measure the cause of it. Folk man sees the world in an illusory perspective. Things which are near to him not only seem large but are thought to be large, and things that are far are thought to be really small. When he thinks of the world at all as a system, he tends to generalize from his own experience. This frequently leads to fallacious views of the world. First, there are fallacies of sampling which arise because the individual's own personal experience is a very limited sample of society as a whole. The classic example of a fallacy of this kind is the remark attributed to Marie Antoinette on being told the people were starving for the lack of bread, "Why don't they eat cake?" The worker in the shop has usually very vague and inaccurate ideas of the life, duties, and responsibilities of the manager. People in the upper class usually have quite fallacious ideas about the life of the lower classes. People in one country have the weirdest notions about the people in another country, and so on.

Secondly, folk knowledge also tends to be subject to the fallacies of composition. There are many things that one man can do because other people are not doing them. If everybody at the same time decided to go downtown, draw money out of the bank or even pay their debts, the whole system would collapse. It is hard, however, to make the jump from personal experience to the system of society as a whole, and it is not therefore surprising that in the folk image of society many fallacies of composition are cherished.

Attitudes toward taxation and the national debt, and attitudes toward national defense, are unusually subject to this kind of fallacy. It is hard for the ordinary man to see that every debt is somebody else's asset, or that every expenditure is somebody else's receipt, and that one country's strength is another's weakness.

A third source of fallacy in folk images of social systems might be called the fallacy of misplaced order. Man has a profound tendency to create an image of order out of apparently random events. The social psychologist Alex Bavelas has reported orally on some experiments in which he gave his subjects a series of random numbers or random patterns and asked them to find the principle by which these sequences or patterns were ordered—without his revealing, of course, that there was no such principle. In all cases the subjects could find some kind of "law," and furthermore, when told there was in fact no law and the material was random in nature they almost invariably became angry and defended the laws which they had discovered with some heat!

It is not only easy for a series of random events to be perceived as a law, but once it is so perceived, if this is difficult to test, the law may actually create its own justification. This is the problem of superstition. If I believe that walking under a ladder will bring me bad luck, then if I have inadvertently walked under a ladder, not only will I be on the lookout for any unfortunate event which might occur but also my frame of mind may be such that I will unconsciously create these unfortunate events, and the superstition becomes actually self-justifying. Both the variety and the persistence of superstition even into advanced societies is testimony to the need for order in the human mind. Man loves to find connections even between the most remote events, and often finds his belief in these connections confirmed because the belief in them biases the observations and even biases the events themselves.

The essential difference between folk knowledge and scientific knowledge, as we saw in the previous chapter, is that whereas folk knowledge draws its inferences from empirical observation, scientific knowledge draws its inferences from theoretical models and from necessary connections. In the language of Hume, folk knowledge is concerned primarily with constant connection whereas scientific knowledge is concerned with necessary connection. If the truth, by contrast with the mere logic of necessary connections, is to be established, there must be an elaborate method of refining, extending, and processing the incoming messages from the senses which constitute the raw material of human perception. In the case of the social sciences the problem of perception is unusually difficult. The reality to be perceived is enormously complex and beyond the range of the sense organs of any single individual. Who, for instance, could "observe" the hundreds of millions of people of India or China? The key to the progress of the social sciences therefore lies in the development of methods of social observation. These methods must avoid the fallacies mentioned above, if knowledge of social systems is to be truly testable and cumulative.

Two methods which have been developed in the social sciences within the last hundred years or so have profoundly improved man's powers of perception of social systems. In this sense they may be compared with the development of the telescope and microscope, which as we have seen had such a profound influence on the perception of physical systems. The first of these methods is the sample survey, by which information can be drawn at relatively low cost from large populations or "social universes" with an approximately known error. An important landmark in the history of any science is reached when it begins to collect information about its own particular universe for its own sake. In the early days of any science its information is largely derived as a by-product of other activities. It only as a science develops its own information processes and control over its information input that it can truly develop a cumulative character. The social sciences only reached this stage in the twentieth century; in many fields, indeed, only within the last generation. Before then information about society was collected as a result of innumerable other concerns and interests, by men of affairs, such as the tax collector, the judge, the military, and so on. Even the early censuses, which perhaps represent the first attempts at deliberate information collection in social systems, were made with highly practical ends in view. In the last generation, however, the method of sample surveys has enormously expanded the basic data about the social system. We might perhaps think of the sample survey as the telescope of the social sciences and depth psychology as its microscope!

The other technique of the social sciences which is almost peculiar to them and which is of great assistance in the perception of complex social systems is the technique of indexing information. This begins in economics with concepts such as the index of the price level or the gross national product. We are beginning to see that the method may be applied to other social and political variables. The significance of this operation is that it enables us to see some essential characteristics of a very large and complex system. It is probably fundamental to all knowledge processes that we gain knowledge by the orderly loss of information. The big buzzing confusion which the world presents to the infant is finally reduced to some kind of perceptual order because we learn to reject most of the information which arrives at the gates of our senses. If a very large amount of information reaches us, the general effect is that of noise. If we are to make the information intelligible we must either filter out the irrelevant or devise some other means of making the relevant stand out. Indexing is a process of filtering out irrelevant information. Thus the gross national product or the general price level is actually an enormously complex vector of millions of numbers. Indexing reduces this vector to a single scalar component. It does this by subjecting reality to considerable violence, and by throwing away a lot of information which in other contexts may be very interesting. It is necessary to do this, however, if we are to perceive the broad outlines of the system.

In the case of economics we can already see the impact on economic policy of social-science techniques in collecting and indexing information. Before the development of an index of general prices, for instance, which did not take place before about 1870, it was possible for quite intelligent people to argue, without either side convincing the other, on the subject of whether prices were rising or falling, or whether there was a problem of inflation or not. Similarly before the development of national income statistics in the 1930's it was possible, say in 1931, for intelligent people to argue about whether there was or was not a depression. With the methods we have at our disposal today it is impossible for either inflation or a depression to get under way for very long without the people who are concerned with policy being aware of the matter. This does not necessarily mean that they will do the right things, but at least the problem will be brought to their attention.

The real significance of the social sciences then is that they open up the possibilities of testing propositions about man and society which previously were thought to be open only for argument, persuasion, or coercion. This is of great importance from the point of view of the resolution of intellectual conflicts. In the natural and biological sciences we have largely eliminated rhetoric as a means of conflict resolution. The attempt on the part of the Victorian bishop, for instance, to resolve the conflicts around evolution by asking Mr. Huxley whether he was descended from the monkeys on his father's or his mother's side, we now regard as a piece of impudent stupidity. The devices of the debater are wholly inappropriate in dealing with questions of physical or even biological systems. We have not yet got to this point in social systems, partly because we still operate so largely in this area by folk knowledge, where the skills of the debater may be an important means of resolving conflict. Over an ever increasing area of social life one hopes that rhetorical dispute is gradually being replaced by reality testing through improved means of perception of social systems.

In religious conflicts, psychological conflict, and political conflict we still find important areas where reality testing is either too difficult or too threatening to be important. In some of these areas reality testing in the social-systems sense is by definition almost impossible. The truth of the doctrine of the transubstantiation of the bread and wine in the Mass in the Catholic Church, by definition, cannot be tested by chemistry, because it is the substance and not the chemical "accidents" which are supposed to be transformed into the body and blood of Christ. Similarly the doctrines of justification through faith, or of sanctification by an emotional experience, as defined in some Protestant denominations, are by definition almost nontestable in scientific terms. Just because a doctrine is untestable does not mean of course that it is unimportant. There are a great many questions, which are important in the sense that they deeply concern man, that are not testable by any ordinary means and perhaps not testable by any means whatsoever. There does seem to be a hopeful tendency, however, in these cases, to develop an agreement to differ, rather than to try to resolve the questions through rhetoric or through violence. This seems particularly true in the matter of religious toleration.

The resolution of conflict about political or social ideologies is more difficult because this often involves fundamental values and principles which people are unwilling to test. Ideological interaction, for instance, between the Communists and the West takes place at an extraordinarily low level of rhetoric. Here, however, the development of abstract statistical rituals of information collecting and processing may eventually get rid of a great deal of unnecessary argument. The question as to which is the best social system for a particular society may not be wholly resolvable through the methods of scientific testing. Nevertheless it seems clear that these methods can substantially reduce the area within which the conflict can be resolved only by rhetoric or by violence. Even though it may therefore be true that political or ideological conflicts ultimately may go back to irreducible differences in fundamental values, it ought to be possible at least for the methods of social science to detect what these irreducible differences are. When this is done much of the conflict may disappear. We shall return to this question later.

IV.

The War Trap

I HAVE suggested earlier that although the great transition from civilization to postcivilization is now under way in many parts of the world, there is no guarantee that it will be completed successfully. I have identified at least three traps which may either delay or prevent the accomplishment of this transition and may even lead to irretrievable disaster and to a total setback to the evolutionary process in this part of the universe. The three traps may be labeled briefly war, population, and entropy. Any one of them could be fatal. Not one of them has to be fatal. And the more self-consciously aware we are as a human race of the nature of the traps that lie before us the better are the chances of avoiding them.

The war trap is the most immediate and urgent. The movement in technology in this area is so rapid that a strong case can be made that this is a problem which must be solved in this generation, for consequences of failure may be fatal. The reason is of course that the scientific revolution and even more the revolution in organized research and development have had a concentrated effect in the field of military technology and weaponry. There has been an enormous increase in man's powers of destruction—at least in the rapidity with which he can employ these powers—and a spectacular increase in the range and deadliness of his deadly missiles. This has created a revolution in the art of war which makes the whole existing political structure of the world dangerously obsolete, and makes the consequences of political breakdown much more serious for mankind than they used to be. A major nuclear war at the present time would certainly be a massive setback, and in view of our ignorance of its ecological consequences it is at least possible that it might be an irretrievable disaster. Furthermore the process of research and development in weaponry which has produced the present situation continues in spite of the nuclear test ban. Most of the major powers are putting resources into research and development of chemical and bacteriological weapons which may easily exceed in ultimate deadliness the more spectacular nuclear weapons. If research and development in weaponry and the means of destruction continue at the rate of the last twenty years, the process would almost certainly lead to the development of what Herman Kahn* calls the "doomsday machine," which will have the power to end all life on earth.

* Herman Kahn, *On Thermonuclear War*, Princeton University Press, 1961.

Under these circumstances the search for stable peace takes on an urgency and an intensity which it has never had before in the history of mankind.

It is probably true, as Toynbee suggests, that war has been the downfall of all previous civilizations. These disasters in the past, however, have been essentially local in character. In some local areas such as Crete or Carthage the setbacks were so severe that the region never fully recovered. For mankind as a whole, with some minor ups and downs, the spread of civilization from its sources in Mesopotamia, the Indus Valley, and Shang China has represented an almost continuous geographical expansion. In spite of barbarian conquests and the destruction by war of many cities, it is doubtful whether the total number of people living in cities has ever declined absolutely for more than a century or two at a time. The character of war has changed so drastically in the last generation, however, that we may well regard the Second World War as the last of the "civilized" wars in spite of the airplane and the A-bomb. The destruction which it caused was largely repaired in less than a generation.

A strong case can be made for the proposition that war is essentially a phenomenon of the age of civilization and that it is inappropriate both to precivilized and postcivilized societies. It represents an interlude in man's development, dated 3000 B.C. to, say, 2000 A.D. It is particularly associated with the development of cities by the expropriation through coercion of the food surplus from agriculture. It is significant that the neolithic villages which preceded the development of cities, in which agriculture was practiced but the surplus from agriculture was not yet collected into large masses to feed urban organization, seem to have been very peaceful. Most neolithic villages, as far as we can judge from the archaeological remains, were unwalled and undefended. Between the invention of agriculture about 8000 B.C. and the first cities of about 3000 B.C. we have the world-wide spread of a remarkably uniform neolithic agricultural culture from its origins in the hills above Mesopotamia west to the extremities of Europe, and east into Asia and the Americas, with Africa south of the Sahara and Australia as the last refuge of the paleolithic hunter. We can hardly doubt that there were many violent encounters between the neolithic farmers and the paleolithic hunters and food gatherers whom they so largely displaced, but these were not organized as war.

With the coming of civilization we have quite a new picture. It is true that by reason of its remoteness the civilization of Harappa and Mohenjo-daro in the Valley of Indus seems to have enjoyed many centuries of peace. These, however, were the remote provincial outposts, and in the center of civilization in Mesopotamia the cities were walled almost from the start. Indeed even before Sumer, Jericho, which may reasonably be claimed to be the oldest city in the world, was a warlike city and itself was destroyed many times. Sometimes as in Egypt an initial period of internal war is followed by the unification of a country cut off from the outside world and a long period of internal peace follows. As contact with the outside world increases, however, the incidence of war once again rises.

This association of war with the urban revolution is no accident. I have suggested that the urban revolution itself is the result of the imposition of a threat system on a society possessing a surplus of food from agriculture. The collection of food from large numbers of farmers and its concentration in the cities is not at first so much the result of exchange as the result of coercion. As suggested earlier, in the first instance the coercion was probably spiritual, and the first city-states seem to have been theocracies. The farmer is threatened with the spiritual disaster if he does not turn over a proportion of his food to the priestly caste. The king, however, soon succeeds the priest as the main organizer of the threat system. Indeed, it was on the alliance of king and priest—that is, of temporal and spiritual coercion—that the urban revolution mainly rests. The concentrated food surplus then enabled the king to organize armies. An army is essentially a movable city. It is an organization quite distinct from mere banditry, raiding, and casual violence, and war is a matter of the interaction of organized armed forces. It requires as its prerequisite the urban revolution—that is, a surplus of food from agriculture collected in one place and put at the disposal of the single authority. Where that single authority is unchallenged from outside, as in favorable situations such as the Indus Valley or the Nile Valley, it might be that a stable system of threat on the part of the ruler and submission on the part of the ruled could be established which would last for many centuries. In more open, less protected, or more thickly populated countries like Mesopotamia the coercion system soon degenerated into war.

The reason for this is very simple. It is due to the fundamental principle that the ability of a threatener to carry out his threat diminishes the farther away from the seat of authority one travels. This is simply because it costs something to transport violence and the means of violence, or even more subtle instruments of doing harm. Like goods, "bads" have a cost of transport. The principle of "the further the weaker" (one should add "beyond a certain point") is an iron law of all organization. The king and the priest can therefore set up a very effective coercive apparatus within the home territory. As they go away from the center, however, eventually they get to the point where their capability of carrying out threats is so diminished that the possibility arises of an independent locus of power. Another king or priest can then arise with a system of counterthreats. Submission is no longer necessary for those beyond the range of the old centers, and so defiance becomes possible. We then get a rival center of power, and the relation between the two power centers is almost inevitably that of counterthreat or deterrence.

A counterthreat system is one in which each party says to the other, "If you do something nasty to me I will do something nasty to you." Such a system may be fairly stable for short periods. But it has a fatal instability. Its stability depends on the mutual credibility of the threats. The credibility of threat is a curious and highly subjective variable of social systems, for it is the credence which I attach to your threat and you to mine that is significant, and this may depend as much on the character of the threatened as on the character of the threatener. Furthermore the credibility of a threat may be only loosely related to the capability of carrying it out, even though there is undoubtedly a relationship of some sort between the two. It is quite possible, however, for one party to be capable of damaging another and for the other not to believe it, or alternatively, I may believe that you have a capability of threatening me which in fact you do not possess. What is clear, however, is that if threats are not carried out their credibility gradually declines. Credibility, as it were, is a commodity which depreciates with the mere passage of time.

In the old days—that is, in civilized societies—capability also frequently depreciated if it was not used. Armed forces, for instance, had a certain tendency to degenerate during peacetime and were re-formed and strengthened during war. This latter phenomenon is less true today in an age of research and development than it was in a cruder and more empirical age. If the credibility of threats in a counterthreat or deterrence system depreciates, however, the time eventually comes when the threats are no longer credible enough to keep the system stable. One party or the other decides that it believes so little in the threats of its potential opponent that it can defy them. When this happens the system experiences crisis. If one threatener is defied the next move in the system is up to him; ordinarily he sees only two choices, either to carry out the threat, which will be costly to him as well as to his defier, or not to carry it out—in which case his future credibility is likely to be impaired. There are possible exceptions to this rule. The failure to carry out a threat the first time it is defied may induce the belief that the threat is more likely to be carried out after a second act of defiance. At some points in this process, however, the threatener is always faced with the grim choice of carrying out the threat or of seeing the whole organization which is based on the threat system collapse, and if he sees nothing to take its place he is likely to carry out the threat at whatever cost to himself or to the defier.

War, therefore, is peculiarly a property of a system of deterrence under urban—that is, civilized—conditions. The cyclic character of war is clearly a product of a system of deterrence which, as we have seen, will be stable for a while but will eventually break down into war. Even from its earliest days, however, the object of war was peace—that is, the re-establishment of a workable and at least temporarily stable system of deterrence again. There are of course a number of different kinds and outcomes of war. There is the limited war characteristic of some periods of history which represents, as it were, the trying out or testing of threat capabilities and the re-establishment of a somewhat revised system of credibilities without much fundamental change in the structure of existing states. The wars of Europe in the eighteenth century, war in almost any feudal age, the wars of the Greek cities before Alexander—or perhaps it would be safer to say before the fall of Athens—were limited war systems.

Sometimes, however, the deterrence system becomes too unpleasant to be stable, and we find wars of conquest and consolidation in which states are actively eliminated. There are also wars of super conquest, such as those of Alexander or of the Roman Empire, which have as their objective the establishment of a world state or at least a state with no challengers. A state which experiences a long series of successes in limited wars may easily get ambitions to be a world state, and if at the same time it comes into the exclusive possession of a superior military technology this aim may be accomplished. In the age of civilization, however, world states were fundamentally unstable, mainly because of the high cost of transportation which constantly permitted the establishment of rival centers of power. The empires of great personal conquerors, Alexander, Alaric, Genghis Khan, and the like, have fallen apart immediately on the death of the conqueror himself. Empires of organization like the Roman Empire have been able to resist the tendency to fall apart over longer periods, as organization can to some extent diminish the cost of transport of military power. But even the Roman Empire was too large for the techniques of its day and eventually gave way to a large number of succession states, as did the Turkish Empire which eventually succeeded it. The instability of empire, the instability of peace, and the cyclical stability of war compose the constant theme of the whole age of civilization from 3000 B.C. to the present time.

I have said earlier, however, that civilization is passing away, and that this is the meaning of the twentieth century. The technical changes introduced by the scientific revolution are so great that we are passing into a new state of man. In this condition stable peace becomes necessary. A world state becomes possible though not necessary, and war becomes so costly and inefficient as a means either of gaining or preserving values that its abandonment is progressively organized. The crucial element in this revolution lies not so much in the increased destructiveness of particular weapons, important as this is, as in the increase in the range of deadliness and the general decline in the cost of transport of the means of violence. The destructiveness of modern weapons is so great and so spectacular that we are apt to exaggerate its importance. The limit of destructiveness is total destruction, and this was reached a long time ago. Babylon, Nineveh, Carthage, and Jerusalem were destroyed just as completely, indeed probably more completely, than Hiroshima or Nagasaki, or even Hamburg and Tokyo. The destruction of cities did not begin with nuclear weapons nor even with high explosives and airplanes. We can now destroy them more rapidly than we used to do, but certainly no more completely.

What is different in the present situation is that we can

effect total destruction at much longer range than we used to be able to do. A system of deterrence will develop, as we have seen, if the capability and the credibility of the threatener diminish rapidly enough with increase in distance from his center so that at some point, say x miles away, a new center of threats can be established and a counterthreat system set up. The question is how far is x. When weapons consisted of battle axes, spears, and bows and arrows in the hands of casual and unorganized tribesmen, their threat capability might decline very rapidly as they moved away from their headquarters. Under these circumstances the city-states could prosper, and the wall around the city reduced the threat capability of potential enemies to negligible proportions within the city boundaries. Even the city-state, however, proved to be unstable the moment the organized army (a guided missile on legs) was invented, even though city-states constantly reappear for short periods in the ebb and flow of military technology and the network of supportive social organizations. It is not quite clear who invented the organized army, but it is plausible at any rate to credit Sargon as the first builder of empire and the welder of city-states into an imperial domain.

Even the organized army, however, had its limits. The farther it got from home the harder it was to feed and organize. Even in the Second World War this principle was important. As Hitler's armies moved into Russia their lines of communication became longer, they became harder to supply, and they became weaker. As the Russians moved back, their lines of communication became shorter and they became stronger. At Stalingrad, at Leningrad, and before Moscow an equilibrium was reached temporarily in a long line where the Germans and Russians were of equal strength. Then the Germans overstrained the resources of the Reich, and German armies were rolled right back into Germany and destroyed. It is clear, however, that any increase in the effective range of the means of violence, whatever these are, is likely to increase the minimum size of the viable state and to diminish the number of such which can coexist.

A further complication in the situation is the existence of projectiles—that is, instruments of destruction which are not carried by hand but are shot to take effect at a distance from the organized armed force. If a state is to be viable in the military sense it must be able to dominate an area around its essential heartland equal in width to the range of the enemy's deadly projectile. Otherwise the enemy can squat within the range of the essential values and shoot at them without ever occupying the territory in person. An increase in the range of the projectile has revolutionized warfare and political relations of states almost as dramatically as an increase in the range of the armies. Thus the invention of the crossbow had a profound effect upon personal warfare, and the invention of firearms an even more striking effect. It has often been remarked that gunpowder destroyed the feudal system even though its foundations had no doubt been weakened by economic factors. Both the feudal castle and the walled city were useless in the face of gunpowder, and new forms of social organization had to be developed to take their place. This is largely a result of the increase in the range of the projectile./

The significance of the military revolution of the twentieth century is that there has been an enormous increase in the range of the deadly projectile and a very substantial diminution in the cost of transportation of organized violence of all kinds, especially of organized armed forces. The range of the deadly projectile, which covered only a few feet or at most a few yards in the days of arrows and spears, a few hundred yards in the early days of gunpowder, a few miles in the beginning of the twentieth century, and a few hundred miles by the time of the Second World War, is now rapidly approaching twelve and a half thousand miles—that is, half the circumference of the earth. This is the end of a long historic process. It cannot go any further than this and be significant. This means, however, that no place on earth is out of range, and the missile and the nuclear warhead have potentially made the conventional national states as obsolete as gunpowder made the feudal baron and the walled city/ By the time of the Second World War it was clear that national states the size of France and Germany were no longer what I call unconditionally viable, as they probably had been even in the early twentieth century. In the Second World War it was clear that the Soviet Union and the United States alone perhaps of all the states of the world retained their unconditional viability, in the sense that they were both large enough for each to be stronger than the other or any likely combination of states at home. France and Germany could be overrun. The Soviet Union could not.

But the developments of the last twenty-five years have profoundly changed the picture. Both the United States and the Soviet Union have the power to do unacceptable damage to each other, and each from points well within their own boundaries. Under these circumstances it is reasonable to assume that unconditional viability has disappeared from the earth and that if we are to retain a world of national states we must all learn to live at each other's mercy. This is not an unprecedented situation. We have in fact had to learn to do this in our personal relations, certainly since the invention of firearms—which had much the same impact on personal viability that the nuclear missile has on national viability. The invention of firearms and perhaps, even earlier, of the crossbow—it is significant that gentlemen never wore crossbows, only swords—led with surprising rapidity to personal disarmament over a very large range of human life and society. Indeed in the modern world a personal threat system backed up by a personal armament survives only in criminal and juvenile delinquent cultures or in remote and undeveloped parts of the world. It is reasonable to suppose that the development of the nuclear missile will have much the same effect on international relations and that it will lead to the abandonment of large-scale organized warfare as an instrument of national policy

just as firearms led to personal disarmament and the abandonment of the use of weapons in personal relations.

It is easy to see that only a system of national disarmament which is close to universal and complete can ensure
stability or even national defense in a world such as we have
today. It is not so easy to see the dynamic steps which will
lead to such a system, nor are we sure what the institutions
will have to be to ensure stability of such a system once we
have arrived at it. The system of general and complete disarmament will be stable if it pays no one to break it—that
is, if it pays no one to rearm. Two conditions may generate
such a situation. The first is where the pay-offs to peaceful
activity are so great that the possible pay-offs of developing
even a one-sided threat system do not look attractive by
comparison. The second is the existence of an apparatus of
law and government which can diminish the pay-offs to one-
sided threats through the invoking of punishment.

The first condition has certainly been an important factor
in personal disarmament. For most of us the gains which we
might have obtained by armed robbery or enslavement seem
very uncertain and meager as compared with the rewards
of participating in the business of peaceful economic development. The second condition—the policeman and the
law—reinforces the first, especially in cases where the first
breaks down.

The same is undoubtedly true these days for nations.
There may have been some economic pay-offs to military
adventure in the sixteenth, seventeenth, and eighteenth

centuries. By the nineteenth century, however, the scientific revolution was so far under way that it began to be apparent that one could get a lot more out of the knowledge of nature than one could out of the exploitation of man. In the twentieth century it is even more apparent that countries which stay home and mind their own business well will get rich, whereas military adventure has a strongly negative rate of return, as the cases of Germany and Japan indicate. Even empire, which is the result of the past military adventure, has become a burden rather than a benefit to the imperial country. Indeed the imperial powers have been getting rid of their empires as fast as they can, with the single exception of poor obsolete Portugal. On the other hand the absence of an effective international policeman and government presents grave dangers where national policymakers have unrealistic images or are emotionally disturbed, so that the first condition is not enough.

The general conclusion of this argument is that man is now faced with the problem of getting rid of war, and this is a unique and unprecedented problem peculiar to the twentieth century. In the age of civilization war was a stable social institution, and for mankind as a whole, a tolerable one. In the twentieth century the system of international relations which was based on unilateral national defense has broken down because of the change in the fundamental parameters of the system, and war has therefore become intolerable. There are many serious thinkers who believe that man is not capable of solving this problem, and that hence he is literally doomed to extinction.

The argument of this chapter, however, permits at least a modest optimism. We have to concede to the pessimists that the probability of irretrievable disaster for mankind within the next few decades, or certainly within a next few centuries, is a positive number. We do not know how large a number this is and one hopes that it is fairly small. As long as it is a positive number, however, no one can feel really secure about the future of himself or of his descendants. We may dramatize the present world situation by saying that every day the hand of fate dips into a bag containing one black ball amid many white balls: the black ball of nuclear disaster. Up to now, every day, fate has brought up a white ball, and the world goes on, but the black ball is still in the bag, and as long as it remains there no one can feel very secure about his future.

On the optimistic side of the picture, however, we have a chance of getting the black ball out of the bag through a learning process. The problem of the abolition of war is essentially a problem in social learning. I know of no theorem which says that man is incapable of this process. As long as he is capable of it, there is also a positive probability that in the future we shall get the black ball of disaster out of the bag of fate. It is this race between learning and disaster which makes the present age so exciting and of such unique significance.

The field of social learning which is relevant to this problem is the process by which man learns to manage his conflicts. It is important to notice that it is the management of conflict and not the elimination of conflict which is the essential problem. If the future of mankind depended on the elimination of conflict the outlook would be black indeed. As long as there is life, there is almost bound to be conflict. Furthermore conflict is not a bad thing in itself. It is indeed an essential element in that creative process by which evolution proceeds. Conflict, however, has a strong tendency to get out of hand and to become destructive. There are well-recognized dynamic processes in the interaction of individuals, organizations, or the states by which conflict becomes intensified. These are the processes involved in arms races, price wars, and mounting tensions and quarrels. These are now better understood than they used to be, thanks in part to the pioneering work of Lewis Richardson in his book *Arms and Insecurity* (Chicago, Quadrangle Press, 1960).

An expression of the same kind of instability in conflict situations is found in game theory under the delightful title of the "prisoner's dilemma." This can be illustrated in terms of the problem of armaments. Suppose we have two countries, A and B. Each can be either armed or disarmed. If both are disarmed both will be better off; call this position 1. They will be richer and more secure than under any other conditions of the system. Unfortunately, however, this happy situation may be unstable. If one country remains disarmed it will pay the other country to arm; call this position 2. Even though this reduces total welfare the armed country may enforce a distribution of this smaller total in its favor, so that it is absolutely better off than before. Either country may take the initiative in this. If, for instance, A arms while B is disarmed (position 2a) then A may be better off than if both are disarmed, but B will be much worse off. In this situation, however, it may pay B to arm, leading to position 3, with both armed. The total welfare will be less than in the second situation, but B may redistribute this diminished total toward himself and so will be better off than he is when he is disarmed and A is armed, although both parties will be worse off when they are both armed (position 3) than when they are both disarmed (position 1.) This presents an almost universal problem in social life, and a great many social institutions have been devised to try to push the system back into the most favorable position (1) and keep it there. The institutions of government, law, police, education, and religion can all be interpreted partly in this light.

Putting the problem in the form of the prisoner's dilemma reveals immediately that there are two lines of attack on its solution. The first is to change the behavior of the parties to conflict themselves, so that they come to take long views and learn to be realistic about the ultimate consequences of their behavior. In the prisoner's dilemma situation, suppose each party is long-sighted so that each realizes that arming unilaterally will benefit him only for a while, and will eventually make him worse off because of the reaction of the other party. Then the initial step from position 1 to position 2 will never be taken. The building in of resistance to short-run temptations because of a long-run point of view is one of the major objectives of moral education, and it is an important element in the whole learning process. Without this, indeed, society would be impossible. The apparatus of law, for instance, would be quite helpless in the face of the widespread individual action to violate it. Law and police operate only at the fringes of society. Unless there is a solid center in which people refrain from taking the short-run advantages of immoral behavior because they have learned to internalize a value system which is based on long-run consequences, the social system could not operate at all. We have seen examples indeed at certain times and places in which the social system has disintegrated into banditry and universal violence, in a Hobbesian war of all against all. In such a situation the mere formal institutions of law, order, and government cannot prevail or even come into being, unless there is a widespread process of moral learning among the individuals of the society by which they learn to moderate their own behavior by social values.

An important and much neglected aspect of the dynamics of a system of this kind is the problem of how a system which moves from position 1 to position 2, in which one party is armed while the other is still disarmed, can be moved back into position 1 instead of going to position 3 of mutual armament. Going back to the terminology of the first part of this chapter, we might say that this problem involves the creative response to threat by which a learning process is set up in the whole system which will eventually restore it to the first position. There are many historical records, for instance, in which the "saint" has overcome the "bandit" and restored him to a place in society. This is perhaps an extreme case, but even at more humdrum level we have developed a large number of techniques which might be described generally as "disarming." The whole history of the rise of politeness needs to be written in the light of this view of social dynamics. The handshake, the bow, the polite form of speech, and the "soft answer that turneth away wrath" constitute a vital part of the techniques of conflict management, yet to my knowledge they have never been recognized as such or given the importance in human history which they deserve.

It is significant that the word civility and the word civil derive from the same root as the word civilization. The age of civilization is characterized not only by conquest, military ruthlessness, and the predominance of the threat as an organizer. It is also characterized by the development of elaborate integrative systems of religion, politeness, morals, and manners. The dynamics of this process whereby the rough feudal baron was turned into a "gentleman"—again the literal meaning of the word is highly significant—is a process that has never been adequately studied, yet it may well be the most important single process in a whole dynamics of the age of civilization, for it is the process which permitted the rise of civil society, without which science would have been impossible. There is a subtle combination of submission and defiance to threat which undermines the threat system itself because it unites the threatener and the threatened in a single integrative social system. This is an art which man has practiced without self-consciousness for thousands of years. It might well be that one of the significant things that is happening in the twentieth century is that man is becoming self-conscious about this process and hence may be able to conduct it more efficiently than hitherto. If this is so it is a genuine source for optimism, for it means that we can set about in a rational and conscious way the elimination of the international threat system which propagates and perpetuates war, and put in its place a genuine system of world integrative relationships.

At the political level this argument may seem strange to us, although it is interesting to see the already enormous development in the twentieth century of what might be called integrative elements in the foreign policies of states—such things, for instance, as cultural exchange, information agencies, even progaganda. As these things are institutionalized they cannot fail to have a profound effect on the behavior of the states themselves. Even propaganda that is initially conceived as an adjunct to the threat system, and that is deliberately and cynically designed to deceive its unwary recipient, may react back on the propagandist, who may eventually come to believe even his own propaganda. Something like this may have happened, for instance, with the

massive peace propaganda which has been put out by the
Communist countries in the last twenty years. Something
which may start off as a hypocritical instrument of national
power ends by taking on a life of its own and profoundly
affecting the value systems of those who have propagated it.
Similarly in the United States, as Gunnar Myrdal pointed
out in *The American Dilemma,* the great moral principles of
the nation as enshrined in the Declaration of Independence, the Constitution, and the Gettysburg Address have
acted with unrelenting pressure in the society to emancipate
the Negro and to bring him toward full citizenship. Where-
ever the professed ideals of a society diverge from its reali-
ties, even though these ideals may be conceived sentimentally
and used cynically, a constant long-run pressure is set up to
bring the reality closer to the ideal.

The ideal of what might be called mature conflict behavior on the part of both individuals and states, or other
organizations, is more important in the modern world than
many have recognized, though the concept has never received a powerful literary expression. In the case of individual behavior, especially in a society moving toward a
universal middle class, the ability to manage conflict without
overt violence and even without undue tension or emotions
of hatred is an important part of the training of the child
and the young adult. The same pattern can be observed in
the businessman, the corporation executive, the government-
al official, or the professional man of the United States, the
equivalent "salary man" of Japan, the manager and com-

missar of the socialist countries, and indeed the middle class everywhere. It is a style of life in which bravado, braggadocio, violence, and even violent emotion are severely frowned upon and lead to rapid demotion. It is a very different style of life from either that of the aristocrat or of the genuine proletariat—both of whom are social species well on the way to extinction in advanced societies. It is therefore not unreasonable to suppose that the learning process which can take place in the individual can also take place in the image of the nation. The ideal of a world of middle-class, nonaggressive, polite states is implied in the behavior of all the more mature countries.

Perhaps one of the greatest short-run dangers to the world at the moment arises out of the fact that the achievement of maturity and political realism on the part of the developed countries has led to the abandonment of empire and hence to the creation of a large number of new countries. Many of these new countries are already exhibiting signs of immature and pathological international behavior. We may therefore have a very difficult period to go through while the new countries "grow up" into political maturity. In this sense, political development may be an ever more urgent task than economic development.

This leads to further consideration of the second element in conflict management which is the development of third-party intervention. We cannot always rely on the learning process or on the dynamics of interaction among the parties to conflict themselves. If the parties in the prisoner's di-

lemma are in fact shortsighted it may be impossible to prevent a deterioration of conflict into a perverse or malign
dynamic in the absence of any third parties. The third party
may play a number of different roles. It may act simply as a
mediator and a teacher, facilitating the learning process by
which the actual parties to the conflict come to manage it
themselves. Third-party intervention, however, usually involves the manipulation of the pay-offs, so that penalties are
imposed on any party which moves unilaterally from position 1 to position 2. A good example of resolution and management of conflict by means of third-party intervention is
to be found in any hierarchy. One of the main tasks of a
person in a superior rank in hierarchy is to resolve the conflicts among his subordinates. He is able to do this partly
because he can act as a teacher, partly because he is part
of an integrative system in which he has status and respect
and in which his words will therefore be listened to and his
advice followed, and also partly because he can employ sanc-
tions—that is, he can make the offending party actually
worse off and so change the pay-offs to the point where it
does not pay any party to move from position 1 to position 2.

This is one of the main functions of the apparatus of law
and police. The criminal by breaking the social contract is
in effect moving society from Position 1 to Position 2. The
apparatus of police and law is set up in order to create a
situation in which crime does not pay. The fact that crime
persists in all societies indicates that this attempt is not universally successful. Nevertheless law and police are usually

successful in confining crime to a small subculture of the
society, and if they did not exist we might find that the
criminal elements would grow so large as to threaten the
stalibity of the society itself.

A successful process of the third-party intervention almost
inevitably involves all these different aspects. Unless the
third party is a teacher in the sense that he affects the behavior and values of the parties to conflict themselves, his
attempt to change the pay-offs is likely to be only partially
successful. On the other hand the lesson of mature, long-
sighted behavior may be too hard to learn or may not even
be true. It may be difficult for these two functions to be
performed by the same body, which perhaps is one reason
why we have developed a large number of para-legal institutions such as arbitration, marriage counseling, social work,
psychiatric care, and the like. It seems that this aspect of
third-party intervention will increase even more in the
future.

The abolition of war then requires a twofold learning
process, one whereby the values and behavior states themselves change toward long-sightedness, toward accurate
reality testing of power systems, and toward a value system
which lays stress on the welfare of all mankind. The other
is a learning process whereby we develop the institutions of
third-party intervention on a world scale. The United
Nations and its surrounding organizations furnish an example. The advocates of world government have a strong
case when they claim that the United Nations is not effec-

tive enough as a third-party organization, and that there
must be a world organization at least sufficiently powerful
to police disarmament and to change the pay-offs of international behavior in such a way as to make an aggression
on the part of any nation obviously unprofitable. We can
then think of the learning process in international systems
proceeding to some threshold on the far side of which we
have a system of stable peace in which the black ball of
disaster has been removed from the bag of fate, and on the
near side of which we have unstable peace and a positive
probability of irretrievable disaster. It seems clear that we
are not yet over this threshold or watershed. Nevertheless
we may be closer to it than we now think. It is uphill all the
way to a watershed, and it has been uphill so long to this
one that we may be excused if we think that the human
road goes on uphill forever. There are, however, watersheds
in social systems, and I believe we are close to this one. It
will therefore be unspeakably tragic if like Sisyphus mankind
falls down the hill again to disaster when he is so close to
the top of this particular divide.

A large part of the solution of any problem is the iden-
tification of the system where the problem lies. In this case
we can put the problem in the form of a change in the
"noösphere," to use a concept of Pierre Teilhard de
Chardin's. The noösphere is the total body of knowledge as
it exists in the three billion minds of the human race spread
over the surface of the earth. The existing noösphere is
almost certainly not consistent with human survival in the

long run, or even in the next few decades. We believe too
many things which are not true, we do not know things that
are true, and we have values (which are also a part of
noösphere) which are inconsistent with the successful management of conflict or the process of human development.
We should not, however, relapse into pessimism on this account, because the noösphere is capable of change and even
of rapid change. An important segment of society which
we are coming to call the knowledge industry is indeed
specifically directed to changing the noösphere, even though
a large part of this activity must be directed toward simple
replacement of the knowledge which is lost by death. In our
day, however, we have a knowledge industry with a capacity
far beyond the mere requirements of replacement, and hence
we can invest in changing the noösphere. This is a process
indeed that has been going on with great rapidity. More
people know more things today than at any other period of
man's history.

The difficulty here is that we do not know in which
direction we want to change the noösphere, and there are
many voices urging change in different directions. The
Communist wants us all to learn Marxism and the planned
economy. A liberal wants us to learn one thing, a conserva-
tive another. In this babel of voices and confusion of con-
flicting remedies the surprising thing is that we make as
much progress as we do.

It is at this point that one hopes that the social sciences
can be of great assistance in the years to come. I have no

illusions about the ability of the social sciences to resolve all conflicts, to reconcile divergent value systems, or to give surefire recipes for salvation. Nevertheless, in so far as the social sciences can provide improved methods of reality testing in the field of social systems, their influence is exerted in the direction of what I will call the survival change that has to take place in the noösphere. The removal of conflict from the area of folk knowledge to the area of scientific knowledge has a stabilizing, one is tempted to say a sterilizing, effect. The hum of the calculator is a great soother of emotions, and calculation, even bad calculation, is the enemy of the irrational. If ideological struggles can be transformed even partially into conflicts of scientific theory, we have a much better chance for their resolution. The whole idea of research in social systems is therefore a stabilizer, and makes actively for successful conflict management.

If I were to nominate the activity which is now open to mankind and which would increase most dramatically the probability of his survival, I would nominate a massive intellectual effort in peace research—that is, in the application of the social sciences to the study of conflict systems and especially of conflict systems in their international aspect. This will be a major part of that self-conscious effort toward the accomplishment of the great transition which is the major task of man in this period of his history.

V.

Economic Development: The Difficult Take-off

IF we avoid the nuclear trap, there are even more difficult obstacles awaiting us down the road. The next one that may confront us is the problem of economic development itself. This has two aspects. The first is the inability of some societies to organize themselves for the transition. This is the difficulty of getting development under way in the first place. The second problem is the general inability of almost all societies to control the growth of population, even those with the most advanced technology. This may soon reduce man to a miserable existence on a hopelessly overcrowded planet. In some societies furthermore, even in the immediate future, their inability to cope with problems of adjustment to an unprecedently rapid rise in population and in the proportion of the young people may prevent them making the transition to a developing economy.

The transition to a developed society is much more, of course, than economic development alone. It involves changes in human personality, in human knowledge, and in virtually all social institutions—the family, the church, the state, the school, the university—as well as in institutions of economic life. Nevertheless economic development is an essential prerequisite and perhaps the most important single part of the great transition. The recipe for economic development is a very simple one. It involves simply devoting a sufficient proportion of the resources of a society to the development process itself. The key concept is that of the growth industry. This may be defined as that part of the total activity of a society which is devoted not to the mere replacement of things and people as they wear out, are used up, and die, but to change, learning, accumulation of goods, and the building of new organizations. It is not easy to define the limits of the growth industry in practice and to say what exactly is in it and what is not in it. A growth industry is spread over all the activity of the society; part of it is found in the family, part in the educational system, part in industrial organizations, and part in government. The concept, however, is fairly clear. In a society without a growth industry or in which the industry is zero, everything as it is consumed or disappears from a society is simply replaced; the whole activity of the society is devoted to replacement. The population is constant, each age group as it passes into the next or as it dies out is replaced by another. The educational process is only just sufficient to replace the loss of knowledge by death and old age. As it wears out, the physical capital of the society is simply replaced by identical objects, the production of everything is exactly equal to its consumption, and hence there is no accumulation and no change. Perhaps no society has ever fulfilled all those requirements, but many societies have been approximately stagnant in this way. Paleolithic society existed for almost inconceivably long periods of time without any substantial change, and even some quite advanced societies seem to have existed for many centuries in a relatively stagnant condition.

The poorer the society the harder it is for it to spare any resources for the growth industry, and very poor subsistence societies are almost condemned to stagnation by the very fact of their poverty. Poverty, however, is not the only explanation of stagnation, and many societies which are rich enough to be able to afford a growth industry have not had one because of the system of values. Where the society's values are unfriendly to change, where a high value is placed upon children exactly reproducing the character and pattern of life of their parents, where formal education is mainly concerned with the preservation of existing knowledge, especially where this knowledge is of purely literary or ceremonial character, and where the state is interested in stability rather than in progress, even a society which is well beyond the limits of subsistence, and even societies which are civilized in our sense of the word, may deny resources to the growth industry and hence be stagnant.

Once a growth industry exists, however, no matter how small, stability is destroyed, and the society cannot help changing. The change may come in many different ways. It may come through change in population at some moment of history. I speculated earlier that a sudden rise in the density of population when the last Ice Age seems to have forced man south into the great Mediterranean "peninsulas" of Mexico, Spain, Italy, Greece, India, Syria and Egypt, and Mesopotamia may have created conditions for growth. At other times a sharp diminution in the population through epidemics, such as took place in Europe at the time of the Black Death in the middle of the fourteenth century, by giving the surviving population a larger living space in land and equipment, seems to have set off a process of development. Some developmental processes seem to have originated in the symbolic systems which are so important in motivating man. The rise of great world religions—among which one should include Communism—has always been accompanied by developmental processes. Sometimes accidental circumstances such as a succession of good crops, or a movement into a new area, have pushed production above consumption for a time and created a surplus out of which further development might grow.

The most important surplus, as we have seen, is that of the knowledge industry—that is, the part of human activity devoted to the increase and dissemination of human knowledge. If the knowledge industry is large enough to create a surplus of production of knowledge over and above what is constantly lost by death and old age, then the society cannot avoid development. Each generation as it matures will know more than its fathers and therefore will be able to do more. A knowledge industry is much more than formal education. It includes all those human activities in the family and in informal groups by which communication increases the total of knowledge in the minds of men. Indeed formal education has often played a negative role in development so far as it has been concerned with purely ceremonial knowledge and the acquisition of status symbols. Even in the early stages of the technological revolution it may be doubted whether formal education played much of a role. The first discoverers and teachers of new technology were often the workmen, inventors, and entrepreneurs themselves. These people might be surprised to find themselves called teachers, but this essentially is their role. The inventor has to teach his invention to others if it is to spread, and an entrepreneur is a teacher of new roles; by creating organizations he teaches people to do things they never have done before, and he usually has to train people in new skills in order to fit them for the new roles in the new organization.

It requires only a slight stretch of imagination to think of the formation of new commodities, new machines, and all new devices as a teaching process imposed on the material world. Every commodity, every machine originates in the mind of man, and its production essentially consists of the process of imposing this image on the structure and arrangement of matter. As the great transition proceeds, of course, formal education and organized research become of increasing importance, for the body of knowledge becomes so large that informal methods of transmitting it and extending it become quite inadequate. It is therefore not surprising that this middle period of the transition witnesses a great increase in the amount of resources devoted to formal education, especially higher education, and also to organized research and development. Indeed, once the early stages are passed the capacity of a society to develop depends very largely on the proportion of its resources which it devotes to formal education and research.

An important question for any society is the role of imports from outside in its development. Some societies have developed almost entirely from their own internal resources without much aid or hindrance from outside. For some other societies their relations with the outside have been crucial in assisting or even in retarding their development. These impulses from outside can be of many kinds. They may simply be imports of information about the outside world which cause a change in the knowledge structure of the society. They may be imports of organization, imports of people of many different kinds—rulers, merchants, missionaries, or workers. They may also be imports of commodities, especially of capital goods. In some cases such as North America, Australasia, and parts of Central Asia within the Soviet Union, this process has been very successful. It has resulted in an autonomous process of development within these areas and has unquestionably brought them into the developing world more easily and with less sacrifice than they could possibly have achieved this status on their own internal resources.

This process, which might be called aided development, often goes through three stages which correspond somewhat to the stages of childhood, adolescence, and maturity in the relation of parents and children. Childhood is the colonial stage in which the developing area imports its government from outside—not always willingly! This is usually accompanied by the import of a great deal of other kinds of organization from the mother country, and there is also likely to be a net import of commodities, especially those commodities which are particularly important to the developmental process. If under these circumstances a process of internal development is set off in the colony, it is then likely to pass into the second stage corresponding to adolescence. In this stage the developing country becomes politically independent but is still economically surbordinate to the previous mother country. This is what the Communists call neocolonialism. The previous colony develops its own political organization but tends to be dependent on the old mother country for much of its economic organization, its foreign trade relationships, and its defense. If the developmental process continues, however, this stage passes over into the third stage of full maturity in which the developing country becomes economically independent of the mother country and stands on its own feet, often repeating the process by becoming a mother country itself. There is nothing necessarily evil in this process. It takes place in all societies, even in socialist societies. Latvia and Uzbekistan are still in the colonial stage with regard to the Russians, Poland is neocolonial, and China is certainly striving to be mature—although this may be premature in the present stage of Chinese development.

While the process of aided development has been successful in many cases, there are also many cases in which it has been unsuccessful. Particularly where colonialism involves the imposition of an essentially alien ruler and alien form of organization on a people, its results can easily be disastrous. In many colonial societies the process of internal development which is necessary before they can pass over to the next stage simply has not taken place, either because of the oppressive government of the colonial power or because of the destructive impact of colonialism on the motivation and the will of the colonial people themselves. Almost everything that happens to the colonial people teaches them that they are inferior. If this lesson is too readily learned it can become tragically self-justifying. There is a decay of morale and the will to achieve in the colonial people which perpetuates the system for generations and arrests the internal development of the colonial territory. Fortunately this is a process which seems to reach its own limits; changes within the imperial power itself, and also external revolutions in other parts of the world, eventually put an end to the colonial status. Very few colonial relationships have lasted for more than three hundred years. The legacy of unsuccessful colonialism, however, is an unfortunate one and may take a long time to overcome.

As we noticed earlier, the decline, indeed what one might almost call the collapse, of colonialism in the twentieth century is a striking phenomenon and it is closely related to the great transition itself. Up to the nineteenth century, at least, it is probable that in many times and places colonialism paid fairly well for the imperial power, whatever it did to the colony. Even before the nineteenth century, however, there are many doubtful cases. It is highly probable, for instance, that the colonies of Spain and Portugal were such a drain on their human resources that they actually prevented the internal development of these countries, which have stagnated and hence become relatively poor countries themselves as a result of their imperial adventures. British colonialism, however, may have paid off for the British in the eighteenth century and French colonialism in the early part of the nineteenth century. But in the latter part of the nineteenth century and especially in the twentieth cenury it became crystal-clear that colonialism in the old sense did not pay the imperial power and that its cost greatly exceeded any returns. For the latecomers—Germany, Italy, and Japan—colonialism was disastrous and the rate of return on their imperial adventures highly negative. By the twentieth century it was obvious that the way to get rich was to stay home and mind one's own business well. In Europe, for instance, the Scandinavian countries and the Swiss, who did not engage in colonial adventures, did better economically than the British, the French, the Belgians, and the Dutch and much better of course than the Portuguese. The significance of the technological revolution is that it makes the exploitation of nature so profitable that the exploitation of man becomes obsolete.

In the light of this fact the collapse of colonialism has an ugly aspect as well as a beneficial one. It does not necessarily arise out of the goodness of heart of former imperial powers. It involves the shifting of a burden and the giving up of responsibility as well as the recognition of the fact that the colonial relationship is corrupting to the imperial powers as well as to the colony. Perhaps one of the greatest dangers we face today, assuming that the East-West relationship can be solved and that the cold war is put in permanent cold storage, is that the developed nations will form in effect an alliance against the underdeveloped, against which the poor countries of the tropical belt will be powerless for many generations to come.

One by-product of the technological revolution is a diminution in the bargaining power of the poor countries as against the rich. The whole impact of technology in these days is toward self-sufficiency of smaller areas. There is a tremendous increase in the number of substitutes for practically everything. The only economic bargaining power which the tropical belt possesses in relation to the developed temperate countries lies in its ability to withhold supplies of tropical products. These, however, seem to be becoming less and less essential to the economic systems of the temperate zone. We now have synthetic rubber, synthetic camphor; synthetic coffee and cocoa may be just around the corner, and the tropical belt may be left with very little in the way of comparative advantage. The only long-run hope for the poor countries would therefore seem to be either the development of a sense of world unity and world responsibility which can outweigh their lack of bargaining power or the development on their part of an internal process of transition independent of external relationships. The first of these is undoubtedly developing—though how much in the way of foreign aid, for instance, is a result of the cold war and would disappear if the cold war disappeared is an open question. The old imperial powers, especially the French and the British, continue to feel a good deal of responsibility for their previous colonies. The Russians, however, have withdrawn substantially from the foreign aid business, and foreign aid is under severe political pressure in the United States. A genuine *détente* between the United States and the Soviet Union might easily have the unfortunate by-product of a sharp diminution in the foreign aid program of both these countries.

The adolescent stage of political development, in which most of the tropical world finds itself, is likewise unfavorable to foreign investment. One can argue, indeed, that foreign investment, if the conditions are right for it, is likely to be much more successful in developing poor countries than any program of foreign aid. People do sometimes get rich by successful borrowing; they rarely get rich by successful begging. The trouble with foreign aid is that there never seems to be enough of it to make any real difference. Nevertheless the breakup of the world into so many independent political units has made foreign investment precarious, and unlikely to develop in any great volume. This again is an aspect of the technological revolution which we have already noticed,—that the highest pay-offs in these days come from staying home and minding one's own business successfully.

There is therefore no escape from the problem of internal development. Indeed, one can assert with some confidence that aided development will be unsuccessful unless there is an internal process of development for it to aid. Aided development, indeed, up to date seems only to have been successful in those countries to which the developed culture has, as it were, been transplanted by migration. The only clear example of successful development outside this area has been Japan, which is a classic example of virtually un-aided development. It is true, of course, that if there had not been an import of information, particularly carried by the messengers of Admiral Perry's battleships, Japan would probably not have organized its own development. Once this information penetrated, however, the development of Japan proceeded almost entirely on its internal resources. In the nineteenth century certainly there was no aid, and there was very little foreign investment. The Japanese themselves went to Europe to learn the new technology, and they themselves took the initiative in importing technology and technicians; and once they had learned the techniques, the foreign technicians were thanked and sent home. The success of Japanese development is due simply to the fact that Japan devoted a substantial proportion of its resources to the growth industry, and particularly to the human resource.

All the law and the prophets of economic development can be summed up in the old proverb that "where there's a will there's a way." The way indeed is absurdly easy and is well known. It consists merely in putting resources into growth. What could be simpler and easier! The problem, however, is the will, and this, I think, we understand very little. The whole cultural milieu of society plays a role in the process of developing its will, and it is hard to separate the determining factors. A widespread puritan ethic, as Max Weber pointed out, is undoubtedly an asset, if this leads people to place a high value on hard work and thrift. On the other hand, puritanism often goes along with a resistance to social change and an unwillingness to innovate outside a narrow field of technology, and thrift alone can often lead to uncreative forms of accumulation or even to unemployment and depression. Mere accumulation is not enough. Economic development does not consist merely in the piling up of things, but in the accumulation of new kinds of things.

Thus, even though the religious and moral ideas which are prevalent in a society and the institutions which embody and propagate these ideas are of key importance in explaining development, it is often hard to put one's finger on just where the importance lies. A puritan ethic is not enough, for there are many tight-lipped societies, like that of the

Highlands of Scotland, which are essentially traditional. On the other hand it is also clear that a hedonistic ethic with no regard to the future is a serious handicap. The grasshopper doesn't build any anthills. On the other hand the ant never gets beyond building anthills. For the will to innovate we must look beyond mere puritanism to what might be called experimental religion, which lays stress on the individual experience rather than on the unquestioning acceptance of ancient tradition. Religious constellations as widely separated as Quakerism and Methodism on one hand and Zen Buddhism on the other may be related to the willingness of the subcultures penetrated by these religious ideas to welcome and initiate change.

By contrast a society dominated by other-worldly, traditional, and static religions, relying on magical formulae, family pressure, and childhood indoctrination for their propagation and popular support, finds development hard. The great problem here is the legitimation of change. In a traditional society change is illegitimate. A traditional religion often plays an important part in creating this sense of illegitimacy of change. Experimental religion legitimates change. On the other hand we might have societies with traditional religion in which, however, the political ideology of the society legitimates change. Both Japan and the Soviet Union may be examples of development proceeding from political rather than religious origins. On the other hand countries as diverse as Spain, Portugal, and Peru in the Christian world and Burma, Ceylon, and Thailand in the

Far East show the difficulties of economic development where a widely prevailing value system derived from religion is traditional, and where the continuing support of a religion depends a great deal on its ability to resist change.

The political problem involved in development can be summed up by saying that development will not take place if those who have the will do not have the power and those who have the power do not have the will. Consequently a political revolution of some sort which removes from power those who do not have the will, and places in power those who do, is often an important prerequisite for development. On the other hand it is not always easy to identify those who either have the will or have the power, and it is not only political revolutions that effect this kind of transfer in society. In capitalist society, for instance, the financial system, especially the banking system, has operated as a constant revolutionary force, putting power into the hands of the innovators and withdrawing power from the traditionalist. The creation of bank credit almost inevitably redistributes the assets of society away from those who engage in familiar and well-established forms of activity and toward those who develop new industries and new commodities, with the aid of new technology. By contrast, however, in some countries a poorly developed financial system dominated by small local moneylenders entrenches traditional ways and prevents development.

We shall examine the role of Communism in development in a later chapter. Here, however, we might note that just as financial institutions may frustrate as well as encourage development, so may the institutions of socialism. When these are applied dogmatically toward areas of economic life to which they are unsuited they can likewise frustrate as well as encourage development. Socialism, for instance, has been noticeably unsuccessful in agriculture, and it is rather unsuccessful in retailing and wholesaling. The success of Communist societies in development has been due to their willingness to put a lot of resources into it, rather than to any efficiency which they have displayed in use of such resources. Even though the recipe for development is therefore a very simple one, the pots in which it can be cooked seem to be almost infinitely varied, and it is the recipe, not the institutional pot, which is important.

One hopes, therefore, that even though the failure of the institutional arrangements in many countries may postpone the onset of development for generations or perhaps even for centuries, this can only be a postponement and not an irredeemable failure. Eventually the example of the developed world will force all societies toward development. A mere desire for development, however, is not the same as an effective will in the hands of those who have the power. But the sheer random shifts in the power structure which take place in all societies must eventually bring into power those who have both the knowledge and the will. From that point on, development is inevitable and irreversible. There are societies indeed in which those presently in power find the price of development too high in terms of the sacrifice of their own prestige and power which it may involve. The developmental process in economics as well as in war and peace may be compared to a watershed or mountain pass. A society may push up the hill toward the pass and fall back many times. Eventually, however, it goes over the top, and that is the point of no return. From then on, the society goes on into a different landscape.

VI.

The Population Trap

ONE of the most difficult problems facing mankind in the present historical era is the control of its own population. The problem has two aspects: an immediate short-run aspect involving the relation of population growth to the dynamics of a developing society, and a long-run aspect involving the ultimate population equilibrium. Both these problems are of great importance and both of them are fundamentally unsolved.

The short-run aspect of the problem is largely the result of the sudden introduction of malaria control and other public health measures in tropical societies which previously have had a high rate of infant mortality. We can regard this if we like as the incursion of certain postcivilized techniques into what are essentially societies in the stage of classical civilization. The results are usually dramatic. With the aid of DDT, it has been possible to reduce the crude death rate from its "civilized" level of about twenty-five per thousand down to nine or ten in a matter of a year or two. The exact physiological causes of this phenomenon are still imperfectly understood. The eradication of malaria seems to be the main contributing factor, though probably not the sole cause. Whatever the cause, however, the facts are clear and the results, alas, can easily be disastrous. There is no more tragic irony than this, that a sudden improvement in the health of the people and especially in the health of children could prove to be a disaster. Nevertheless in the absence of an equally sharp decline in the birth rate these societies may easily find themselves faced with an unmanageable problem which may actually prevent their economic development altogether.

The problem arises because a sudden change in infant mortality, without a corresponding change in the birth rate, results in a shift in the age distribution of the society toward the younger ages with great rapidity, so that they have an unusually large proportion of children. This means correspondingly that the proportion of the population of working age is diminished. Thus in 1955 the proportion between the ages of fifteen and fifty-nine was an almost uniform 61 per cent in Europe, North America, and Oceania—that is, the developed part of the world—whereas in tropical Africa it was only 49 per cent, and in Asia about 55 per cent. This is in spite of the fact that in the developed part of the world there is a much larger proportion of old people. In Africa and Southeast Asia 43 per cent of the population were under the age of fifteen. In part this is due to adult mortality, so that a smaller proportion of the population live to be sixty. In part it is also a result of the tremendous decline in infant mortality which hit most of these countries in the late 1940's.

This situation, in which infant mortality declines without a corresponding decline in the birth rate, and before an expansion of adult longevity, is a recipe for demographic and economic disaster. A constantly declining proportion of the population of the working age has to support the constantly increasing proportion of population of nonworking age, and the ability of the society to spare resources for a growth industry is correspondingly impaired. The problem is made doubly difficult because a major element in the growth industry itself is the education of the young. When there is a very large proportion of children and young people, it becomes increasingly difficult to provide the resources for the kind of education which is necessary if the society is to pass over into the modern world.

One of the essential differences between civilized and postcivilized society is that in civilized society a relatively small proportion of resources of the adult working population need to be devoted to the upbringing and education of the young. Children are raised and educated in the casual spare time of their mother, whose time mainly has to be devoted to the productive work of the peasant farm, the small shop, or the industrial household. In a postcivilized society the amount of learning which must be performed by the average individual is so great that the task of education cannot possibly be done by the family. There therefore has to be an increasing proportion of resources devoted to formal education, and as we move toward postcivilization we move toward a society in which virtually every child and young person receives formal education for the first twenty years or so of his life. This deliberate investment in the human resource is the main key to the transition from civilized to postcivilized society. And in those civilized societies which are suffering the great demographic upheaval the problem of the transition is enormously intensified because of the burden of the large proportion of children.

For the developed countries the dynamic problem of the demographic upheaval is not so severe, though even in many of these countries the remarkable upsurge in the birth rate from about 1940 on has created a serious problem for education. All countries, however, whether developed or undeveloped, face the problem of long-run equilibrium of population. There is no country in the world whose population is stationary. The average rate of increase of the world population at a very modest estimate is about 1.6 per cent a year, and over the next forty years this may be 2 per cent a year. This means a doubling of the world population in something under forty years. It is little wonder that the present century is called the age of population explosion. In the whole of its history the human population has never expanded at this rate, and it is clear that this rate of expansion cannot go on for very long. At present rates of population expansion it will take only a little over three hundred years for a whole land area of the world to become a single city. It takes only seven or eight hundred years before we have standing room only over the whole face of the planet! Just in case anyone thinks we can solve the problem by shooting people to outer space, it would take only about eight thousand years at the present rate of population increase before the whole astronomical universe, two billion light years in diameter, is packed solid with humanity!

A generation ago it seemed reasonable to suppose that this problem would solve itself with the increase in income. It was observed that the richer countries had lower birth rates than the poorer countries and that the richer classes within each country had a lower birth rate than the poorer classes. The recipe for the control of population then seemed merely to be to make everybody rich. Then it was argued that people would become aware of the high cost of having children and would automatically restrict their families to the numbers which would not diminish their income. In the 1930's, indeed, there were many areas in Europe and many sections of the population in North America where the net reproduction rate was so low that there was a fear of race suicide. The net reproduction rate may be roughly thought of as the ratio of each generation to the numbers of its parents. If this ratio is one, then each generation as it dies off leaves an exactly equal generation to replace it. If it is more than one, the population is bound to increase; if it is less than one, the population is bound to diminish. In the 1930's in many parts of the developed societies the net reproduction rate was actually less than one. In the 1940's, however, there was a change, perhaps caused by rising incomes, coupled with a more favorable attitude toward children. This may signify a retreat into the family as the one island of security in a world in which the state has become a monster incapable of providing security or of attracting true affection. Whatever the reasons, the facts are clear. In almost all societies today, the net reproduction ratio is much greater than one. At its present rate of increase, for instance, the United States will reach a billion people in a little over a hundred years. It is therefore quite possible that our great-grandchildren will look back on this as a golden age of spacious living and will inhabit a planet in which there is no room to move and no place to go.

Mankind is therefore faced with a hideous problem in terms of sheer arithmetic. It is an arithmetic, moreover, which cannot be denied even though we nearly all try to deny it. The arithmetic is simply this: *any* positive rate of growth whatever eventually carries a human population to an unacceptable magnitude, no matter how small the rate of growth may be, unless the rate of population growth can be reduced to zero before the population reaches an unacceptable magnitude. There is a famous theorem in economics, one which I call the dismal theorem, which states that if the only thing which can check the growth of population is starvation and misery, then the population will grow until it is sufficiently miserable and starving to check its growth. There is a second, even worse theorem which I call the utterly dismal theorem. This says that if the only thing which can check the growth of population is starvation and misery, then the ultimate result of any technological improvement is to enable a larger number of people to live in misery than before and hence to increase the total sum of human misery. These theorems can of course be restated in a cheerful form—that if something other than starvation and misery can check the growth of population before it reaches an unacceptable magnitude, then the population does not have to grow until it is miserable and starved. The cheerful forms of these theorems, however, require work and conscious effort and social organization. In the absence of these, the dismal theorems take over.

For the theorems to be cheerful we must face another piece of arithmetic. This is, that in an equilibrium population the birth rate and death rate must not only be equal, but must be equal to the reciprocal of the average age at death—or what is the same thing, of the average expectation of life at birth. If the average age at death is twenty-five, then the birth rate and the death rate will be forty per thousand in an equilibrium population. If the average age of death is seventy, as it will be in a postcivilized society, then the birth rate and the death rate cannot be more than about fourteen. If there is no birth control—that is, the limitation of the number of births below the natural limit of fecundity—then there can be no death control. If the birth rate is allowed to rise to the limit of natural fecundity, which is something between forty and fifty per thousand, the death rate will also eventually rise to this level, and this means that the average age at death will be only twenty-five years or even less. This indeed is the typical condition of classical civilization. If we want to have death control, and if we want to raise the average age of death to seventy, then we must face the limitation of birth. Any moral principle which states otherwise is false morality, for no morality can be true which attempts to deny the sheer fact of arithmetic.

Having said this, we must hasten to add that there are many different methods of achieving limitation of births. Contraception is one method and an important one but by no means the only one, and indeed it is almost certainly not sufficient. As in the case of economic development, the motto in population control seems to be "where there's a will there's a way." The will is all-important, the way is secondary. Many of the ways, however, which are most effective are also unpleasant and indeed unacceptable. Infanticide and abortion are probably still the most certain methods of population control. Infanticide is repugnant to a developed moral sensitivity and can hardly be practiced without destroying certain intangible values which are important to a high quality of human life. Abortion is undoubtedly preferable to infanticide, though we know too little about the physiological and psychological damage which it may cause to recommend it without serious qualms. If this is the only method for successful population control, however, the moral prejudice against it may have to be waived in the light of the unmitigated human misery which will result from inability to control population altogether. This is one place where we have to reckon the moral cost against the moral returns.

Contraception certainly seems preferable to abortion, and indeed the moral objection to contraception in principle seems to be confined to a single major branch of the Christian church. Even here the difference in practice between this church and the rest of society is much smaller than the difference in precept. Contraception, however, also has its problems, and it is by no means an automatic solution to the problem of population control. Even with full knowledge and practice of contraception parents may still decide, voluntarily, to have more children, on the average, than are required to keep the population in a stable equilibrium. Furthermore existing methods are by no means certain in operation, and even if, for instance, most parents decide to have two children but end up by accidentally having a third, this is enough to upset the population equilibrium.

The fact that we must recognize is that it is social institutions which are dominant in determining the ability of a society to control its population, not the mere physiology of reproduction. A classic example of this proposition is Ireland. The Irish learned the Malthusian lesson the hard way. In 1700 they had a population of about two million. They were living in misery on small grains. Then someone introduced the potato, which was a great technical improvement, enabling a larger amount of food to be grown per acre, and indeed per man, than before. For a while the standard of life of the Irish improved, infant mortality declined, and there was a great increase in population. By 1846 there were eight million people living in misery on potatoes. Hardly any better example of the utterly dismal theorem can be found. Then came the failure in the potato crop and the great famine. Two million people died of starvation. Two million emigrated and the four million who remained had learned a lesson. The population of Ireland has increased very little in over a hundred years, partly as a result of continued emigration, but more as a result of limitation of births. In this case the limitation was achieved through late marriages and the imposition of a strongly puritan ethic upon the young people which seems to have the effect of strongly limiting the number of children born out of wedlock. It is striking that one of the most successful examples of population control should have taken place in a Roman Catholic country, one, however, in which Catholicism takes an unusually puritanical form.

But the great variety of possible solutions to this problem becomes apparent when we look at Japan, which is almost the only other country where the deliberate limitation of population growth has had much success. Here the machinery of population control seems to have been abortion rather than late marriages. The precariousness of these solutions, however, is indicated first by the fact that neither of them has been totally successful, for in neither Ireland nor Japan has the net reproduction rate actually been reduced to one, and in the second place even the existing solutions can easily break down under the impact of social change or economic development.

On a world scale this whole problem is enormously complicated by the different rates of population growth of different regions and nations. The first fruits of the technological revolution were enjoyed by Europe, and the period from 1500 to the early twentieth century can well be regarded as dominated by the expansion of European power and European populations to other parts of the world. The entire continents of North and South America and Australia were in fact populated largely from Europe, at least in their temperate regions. The mosquito saved most of tropical Africa from European immigration, and Asia was already reasonably full of people at the beginning of the era. We now find ourselves in the twentieth century with this period of expansion come to an end and very few open spaces left in the world. The geographical distribution of the world population is probably set for a long time to come, excluding wars of biological extermination.

Under these circumstances the problem of migration as a solution to the population problem becomes one of great difficulty. It is clear that migration is no longer a general solution for the population problem, and indeed on a world scale may actually intensify it. A region which is under genuine Malthusian pressure, for instance, can easily become a perpetual source of emigrants. If the population is really being limited by the food supply, then every person who emigrates releases food which enables another child or even two to survive. Even in the relatively short run, migration then provides very little alleviation of severe population pressure. Furthermore emigration often has a bad qualitative effect on the society which is losing people in this way, for it is usually the young, the ambitious, and the energetic who migrate. Hence in a society which has a substantial volume of emigration it is the old, the children, the sick, and the unambitious who remain behind not only to carry on the work of the society but also to produce the next generation. A society or a region which has a long-continued emigration therefore becomes depleted in human resources. It usually lacks leadership and sometimes becomes completely incapable of reorganizing itself. The southern Appalachian region in the United States is a good case in point. In these societies even the education system often turns into a funnel to drain off all the best young people, and so benefits the society which is receiving the migrants rather than the one that is educating and then losing them. The tragic truth of the principle that "to him that hath shall be given" is dramatically illustrated by this principle. The rich areas or the rich countries tend to attract the abler people from poorer areas, and this perpetuates or even increases the disparities of income.

The different rates of growth of different populations also comprise an important long-run force producing international and internal political tension. The idea of population pressure as a cause of war is too crude to be taken very seriously. Population pressure itself is a result of a large number of social factors some of which may increase and some of which may diminish the propensities to make war. Nevertheless differential rates of population growth unquestionably increase the difficulty of the problem of stable peace. The unwillingness of many countries and many subgroups within countries to face the problem of population control is closely connected with their unwillingness to seem to weaken their relative position in the world. The inability of the United Nations, for instance, even to get this problem on its agenda is a reflection of the fact that the fears of relative changes in population are sufficient to prohibit any rational discussion of the total problem.

Ability to handle this problem intelligently is further handicapped by the fact that there are some short-run exceptions to the principles outlined above. The example of Puerto Rico, for instance, suggests that in a poor, small country which is already suffering from severe population pressure the ability to find a temporary outlet for its surplus population can be an important aid in its development. Certainly if Puerto Rico had not been able to send over half a million people to the mainland of the United States its development over the last twenty-five years would have been much more difficult. It is therefore hard to say to a country like Haiti or Indonesia or even China, "You must not export your surplus population, for this will do you no good in the long run." Indeed if a process of internal reorganization is going on, this proposition may not be true. It is not even always true that an increase in population is an enemy of development. There are some societies indeed in which population increase is the first step toward development. A decline in infant mortality upsets the old family structure, tends to destroy the extended family, provides a labor force for new cities, and may indeed provide precisely the disequilibrating influence which will throw the society off its old equilibrium of stable poverty and create an ongoing process of development.

It is very hard to avoid a certain pessimism in this area. Nowhere are such strong forces laid against the learning of realistic images of the future of mankind. All existing solutions to this problem are either disagreeable or unstable, and yet solutions must be found if postcivilized society is not to end in disaster and if our great technological accomplishments are not to result in enormous increase in the total sum of human misery. There is need to devote a substantial intellectual resource to this problem, and this we are not doing. We need to expand our knowledge of physiology, psychology, sociology, economics, and ethics in this whole area. There is a strong temptation for "folk wisdom" to refuse to face this problem or to try to brush it off with partial solutions. The Communist and the Catholic are curiously alike, though for different ideological reasons, in this particular respect, and they both seem to be almost incapable of developing a realistic appraisal of the nature of the problem and the need for its solution. On this particular point my perception of truth requires me to say that I think both the Communist and the Catholic are, at present, enemies of man's future, although I think it is also possible for both of them to reform and to take a more realistic attitude. I am deeply conscious furthermore that the "liberal" attitude toward the subject, while it may recognize its importance, has contributed very little toward its solution. We are all guilty of ignorance, frivolity, and blindness, and the accusing fingers of billions of the unborn are pointed angrily toward us.

I have only one positive suggestion to make, a proposal which now seems so farfetched that I find it creates only amusement when I propose it. I think in all seriousness, however, that a system of marketable licenses to have children is the only one which will combine the minimum of social control necessary to the solution to this problem with a maximum of individual liberty and ethical choice. Each girl on approaching maturity would be presented with a certificate which will entitle its owner to have, say, 2.2 children, or whatever number would ensure a reproductive rate of one. The unit of these certificates might be the "deci-child," and accumulation of ten of these units by purchase, inheritance, or gift would permit a woman in maturity to have one legal child. We would then set up a market in these units in which the rich and the philoprogenitive would purchase them from the poor, the nuns, the maiden aunts, and so on. The men perhaps could be left out of these arrangements, as it is only the fertility of woman which is strictly relevant to population control. However, it may be found socially desirable to have them in the plan, in which case all children both male and female would receive, say, eleven or twelve decichild certificates at birth or at maturity, and a woman could then accumulate these through marriage.

This plan would have the additional advantage of developing a long-run tendency toward equality in income, for the rich would have many children and become poor and the poor would have few children and become rich. The price of the certificate would of course reflect the general desire in a society to have children. Where the desire is very high the price would be bid up; where it was low the price would also be low. Perhaps the ideal situation would be found when the price was naturally zero, in which case those who wanted children would have them without extra cost. If the price were very high the system would probably have to be supplemented by some sort of grants to enable the deserving but impecunious to have children, while cutting off the desires of the less deserving through taxation. The sheer unfamiliarity of a scheme of this kind makes it seem absurd at the moment. The fact that it seems absurd, however, is merely a reflection of the total unwillingness of mankind to face up to what is perhaps its most serious long-run problem.

VII.

The Entropy Trap

ENTROPY is a term which originated in thermodynamics. It measures the ability of a system to perform work or activity in the future. It was originally defined in a curiously negative way so that as the potential ability of a system declines entropy increases. A system with no entropy has a lot of potential and a system with high entropy has little. The famous second law of thermodynamics states that as work is performed entropy increases—that is, the potentiality for the performance of further work declines. Energy, in other words, becomes less and less available to do work. The principle can easily be generalized for all systems. All systems begin with a potential for activity. As activity is carried out, however, this potential is used up, and eventually the system comes to a point of equilibrium at which all potential is used up and no further activity can take place.

The second law of thermodynamics can therefore be

generalized under the name of the principle of diminishing potential. This principle takes many forms both in physical and biological and in social systems. In simple thermo-dynamic systems, for instance, work can be performed and thermal energy transformed into mechanical energy only if there is a difference in temperature between two parts of the system. The transformation of thermal into mechanical energy, however, always diminishes the temperature differ-ences and hence diminishes the potential for further work. Similarly water at the top of a hill can perform work by running downhill and turning mills and turbines. Once it is at the bottom of the hill, however, its capacity for further work is exhausted. Electric current likewise can perform work only if there is a potential difference between two points. The performance of the work, however, diminishes this potential difference.

The process of aging in a biological system likewise seems to be akin to the using up of potentials. The fertilized egg has an enormous biological potential; the old person, very little. The social system likewise exhibits a tendency to run down. Corporations, churches, and empires originate in an outburst of social potential in a form of an entrepreneur, prophet, or conqueror. In the course of time, however, this potential is used up and eventually the organization which it created disintegrates. The similarity with the aging process in biological organisms is very striking, though this analogy, like all analogies, should not be pushed too far. There is therefore a kind of thermodynamic dismal theorem which sees the end of the universe as a uniform soup in which the absence of any differentiation and the dominance of an all-pervasive uniformity make any kind of further activity impossible. All things will be at the same temperature, all matter will be evenly distributed, and nothing more can happen.

The process of evolution seems at first sight to run contrary to the general principle of diminishing potential. We are dangerously close to some metaphysical shoals at this point, and we must turn quickly away from some fascinating but unanswerable question about the origin and the end of the universe. What we see in the evolutionary process, however, may be described as the use of energy to segregate entropy. Entropy can also be thought of as a measure of chaos—which may be defined, oddly enough, as the most probable state of any system. Negative entropy can then be thought of as measuring the degree of organization, structuring, or improbability of a system. Evolution moves the world toward less probable and more complicated arrangements, system patterns, and structures, whether in biology or in society. Thus even though the principle of diminishing potential is moving the universe as a whole toward increasing entropy and increasing chaos, the evolutionary process operates to create more order at some points at the cost of creating less order elsewhere. This is what I mean by the segregation of entropy.

The evolutionary process seems to have started with some kind of fertilization or creation of potential in the universe in the primordial cosmic explosion and then proceeded to the creation of the elements, of increasingly complex compounds, amino acids, proteins, viruses, and eventually life. Life develops increasingly complex forms, eventually producing man; man creates language and society and begins the process of social evolution which again proceeds to develop increasingly complex forms. The universe then is seen to be like a man, who is spending his capital so that his total capital in the form of potential continually diminishes, but who continually builds up the diminishing capital into ever more elaborate works of art. Thus when a sculptor makes a statue out of a piece of stone, there is more organization in the statue than in the stone, in the sense that the shape of the statue is much less probable than that of the stone. But if we look at the whole system, the stone, the statue, the chips, and the sculptor himself, we shall find that the organization of the statue has been bought at the cost of disorganization in the chips and perhaps in a diminution of the potential of the sculptor.

The key to the evolutionary process, whether in biology or in society, lies in a set of related phenomena associated with teaching, learning, and printing. This indeed is the secret of the enormous evolutionary potential of life. The gene operates as a three-dimensional printer, for it has the ability to produce exact copies of itself in the material world. Printing is a process by which order can be copied and spread. When a teacher teaches a class, furthermore, the students know more at the end of the hour and the teacher knows no less. Indeed, by a process which is even more mysterious, the teacher knows more too. The impact of man in the evolutionary process arises because of the capacity of his images—that is, the knowledge present in his mind—to grow by a kind of internal breeder reaction: the imagination. It is this which has given the human nervous system such a fantastic social-evolutionary potential, a potential of which we have probably hardly used up 1 per cent in the brief history of the human race.

Turning now to social and economic systems, we find that the entropy problem manifests itself in a number of forms. The most obvious of these is perhaps the diffusion or concentration of material. We can distinguish between entropic processes which diffuse concentrated material and anti-entropic processes which concentrate diffused material. Mining is the best example of an entropic process, and a considerable part of our economic life at present consists of taking concentrations of ores, fossil fuels, and minerals and diffusing these or the products of their combustion or manufacture over the surface of the earth, the oceans, and in the atmosphere. We take coal and oil from the earth and burn them, thus reducing them to chemically less available substances like carbon dioxide—which is then diffused throughout the atmosphere and the oceans. We take iron ore from the mines, manufacture it into iron and steel, and eventually diffuse these products in innumerable dumps and fragments of rust over the surface of the earth. We take phosphates and potash from mines and from soil, build these into foodstuffs, and finally excrete them into the rivers and eventually into the oceans.

This process of diffusion obviously cannot go on forever, and one can take a dismal view of economic development as that process by which the evil day of exhausted resources is brought all the nearer. In terms of geological time all known accumulations of ores and fuels will be dissipated in a flash. Even in terms of man's own history, at present rates of consumption the known reserves will be largely exhausted in a mere matter of centuries. It may therefore be that the present period will be seen as a very brief episode in which man managed to maintain a high-level society over a part of the earth at the cost of an enormous increase in human population and the rapid exhaustion of his geological capital, and that even in a thousand years—a brief period even in human history—our descendants will inhabit an exhausted and ravaged earth from which all mineral deposits and all fossil fuels have been irretrievably removed. Man will then be pushed back into a low-level society, scratching a miserable living once again from the fields and the woods.

Fortunately there are signs that this vision is too dismal and that an anti-entropic technology is on the way—that is, one which will concentrate diffused material rather than diffusing the concentrated. It may well be that when the history of this century is finally written the wars and revolutions will recede into the background as mere unimportant disturbances from a long-run point of view; and the great events of the century will be seen to be such developments as the Haber process, which concentrates nitrogen from the diffused atmosphere into fertilizer and explosives, and the Dow process, which concentrates the metal magnesium from the illimitable resource of the sea.

Furthermore, space technology is forcing us in the direction of what have been called closed-cycle human systems in which a group of human beings sustain and reproduce themselves endlessly by a circulation of a closed cycle of materials. In the spaceship of the future and perhaps even in the household on earth man will be part of a small closed cycle of material flow, growing his food from his own waste products and possessing a self-reproducing structure of material environments. Even if this problem should be proved to be insoluble for small groups, it is quite possible to visualize an earth of the future which has a stable closed-cycle technology dependent upon the atmosphere and the sea as the basic resources from which diffused elements are concentrated and to which the concentrations are eventually returned. Man will then be independent of geological capital. We can therefore regard the present period as a unique opportunity in the history of this particular planet whereby the geological capital which has been accumulated over hundreds of millions of years in the form of ores and fuels can be spent to produce enough knowledge to enable man to do without the geological capital which he exhausts.

The materials problem is not the only one. There is a further problem of energy. We can conceive a closed-cycle economy in a material which simply circulates from one form to another. We cannot, however, conceive a closed-cycle economy in energy. We can prevent the increase of entropy and the rise of disorganization in the system only by the import of energy from outside. The development of nuclear energy and especially the possibility of thermo-nuclear energy have enormously extended our horizons in this regard. It may indeed be that nuclear fission will prove to be impractical as a long-run source of energy because of the disorganization involved in the production of waste radioactive products. Fusion does not seem to have this handicap to such an extent, though of course the energy of fusion is much more difficult to control. However, man's ability to control nuclear energy usefully is almost certain to increase, and even if this does not solve the problem, the import of energy from the sun to the earth may be considered as inexhaustible as far as man's tenure of the planet is concerned, and it will be very surprising if we do not soon greatly increase our ability to use this import of solar energy. The energy problem therefore may be less serious than the materials problem, though we should by no means assume that it has already been solved.

A more subtle problem of which we should certainly be aware, although in the present state of human knowledge it is hard to see what we can do about it, is the problem of the possible exhaustion of man's biological potential. Many people have been worried whether the development of high-level society with its consequent preservation of many genetically defective human beings would not result in progressive genetic degeneration of the human gene. In the present state of knowledge we do not even really know whether this is an important problem or not, so it is hard to mobilize much human intelligence to solve it. The possibility, however, of a dismal theorem in genetics should not be ruled out altogether. It may be, for instance, that the present dramatic improvement in human health and in the expectation of life is only a temporary gain, and that the unfavorable genetic result of such a system will eventually force us back into something like the old equilibrium again, with the expectation of life again only 25–30. Furthermore the human race seems to have exhausted its purely biological potential in the sense that almost all possible mutations of man's genetic structure seem to be unfavorable.

One does not have to go to genetics, however, to perceive a problem of social entropy in man's own nature and constitution and in the social organizations which he creates. Man is a highly improbable being and he constantly tends to slip down into more probable and less highly organized states. This indeed is the physical meaning of death. His own constitution, therefore, and the societies which he creates are precarious, in the sense that their equilibrium, maintenance, and development require constant vigilance, attention, and work. The "prisoner's dilemma" problem mentioned in Chapter IV is a good example in social systems of the principle of entropy. It requires work to keep the social system at peace and to prevent it from slipping down into arms races and mutually destructive violence.

Social movements as well as commodity movements can be classified either as entropic or anti-entropic. There are those which tear down and those which build up. In the present state of the world, for instance, it is very easy for nationalism and nationalistic movements to become entropic—that is, to destroy world order in the supposed interest of preserving national order. Religious and political movements, in so far as they appeal to the legitimation of hatred and the displacement of aggression on the unbeliever and the heretic, are likewise entropic. We still do not have social inventions and machinery which are capable of dealing with dangers of this kind. We still have a world in which future Hitlers and Stalins can create enormous misery for mankind, and we have very few defenses against such possible perverse movements.

It is interesting to observe how the highest principles of morality and those attitudes and institutions which have been regarded as expressing a high morality are usually anti-entropic. It is at least a useful first approximation of the problem of moral value to suppose that the highest test of a value is whether it performs an entropic or anti-entropic function in society. On this principle, love, in the sense of the Greek *agape*, emerges as the most anti-entropic of all human relationships. It always builds up, it never tears down, and it does not merely establish small islands of order in society at the cost of disorder elsewhere. It is hard for us, however, to learn to love, and the teaching of love is something at which we are still very inept. The process of moral learning is a long uphill climb, and the hill seems to get steeper and slipperier as we climb it.

A troublesome question, which is again worth asking even though we cannot answer it, is whether man needs a certain amount of trouble, difficulty, challenge, or even pain in order to stimulate him to that constructive activity which is necessary to prevent him from going to pieces. In a sense this is the analogue in the social system to the problem of the genetics of degeneration in the biological system. The basic problem, to which we have as yet very imperfect answers, is how evolutionary potential is generated. This is something we do not understand even in biology. Why is it, for instance, that certain lines of evolutionary development seem to reach a dead end with all the evolutionary potential exhausted, whereas other lines go on to ever increasing differentiation and complexity? It may well be that evolutionary potential always emerges out of some kind of crisis situation, and that without catastrophe of some kind evolutionary potential would soon be exhausted.

There seems to be a conflict here between adaptability and adaptation. Up to a point these qualities seem to be competing goods both in biological and in social structures. There are some biological organisms and some social organizations which adapt themselves extremely well to a particular environment and which therefore flourish exceedingly as long as this environment remains. If all environments were stable the well-adapted would simply take over the earth and the evolutionary process would stop. In a period of environmental change, however, it is the adaptable not the well-adapted who survive. These are the periods when the meek can inherit the earth, and it is meekness— that is, adaptability—which seems to carry the greatest evolutionary potential. We may therefore worry whether the end results of the great transition will not be to create an environment for the human race so stable, so free from catastrophe, and so free from environmental change of all kinds that human adaptability will degenerate, not so much because man has adapted to his environment as because he has made his environment adapt to him.

Some confirmation of these gloomy predictions may be found in the history of leisure classes in many different civilizations. We can think of the leisure class in a civilized society as being that small proportion of society which has achieved in a sense a postcivilized standard of life. In post-civilized society this standard of life is extended to all men, and the very poorest and meanest has the capability of living like a Roman emperor. The Roman emperors, how-ever, while they all may have lived luxuriously, rarely lived virtuously. It is all too easy to visualize a postcivilized world of besotted hedonists with wires running into the pleasure centers of the brain, enjoying enormous but meaningless sensations of rapture in a totally stable and unchallenging mechanical environment. Such a world would lose its adapt-ability to the point where a very slight worsening of the over-all environment might destroy it. The most successful leisure classes and the ones which have maintained their vigor the longest seem to have done so by practicing a set of artificial miseries and discomforts such as fox-hunting, dressing for dinner, opera, court ceremonial, and athletic games. Therefore if the human race is to prevent itself from disintegrating through sheer boredom or lasciviousness in a postcivilized society, it may be necessary to introduce artificial discomforts, and it may be hard to do this when comfort is so easily attainable. The ideal is of course to find a way in which comfort and virtue can go hand in hand, but so far we do not seem to have been too successful in finding this happy combination.

These problems may be hard to solve but I know of no proposition that says they are insoluble. We may, indeed, be very close to the solution of the problem of material entropy and continued energy import. Unfortunately at the moment we do not know two things which vitally affect man's future. We do not really know how far we are from a stable, closed-cycle, high-level technology. And we do not know how many people such a stable technology would support.

It may be that the solution of the material and physical problems is just around the corner. It will not be surprising if the next fifty years bring some major advances, both toward new and practically unexhaustible resources of energy and also toward anti-entropic modes of organizing the flow of materials into and out of the necessary physical components of man's environment. The uncertainty in the movement toward stable, high-level technology, however, makes one all the more resentful of the waste of resources involved in the world war industry and in frivolous and useless consumption. It may be that man has only a slim chance of achieving a stable, high-level technology and that every gram of material or dyne of energy that we waste and that is not directed toward making the great transition is an appreciable diminution of the probability of making it. On the other hand it is also possible that stable, high-level technology is within easy reach and we will attain this while we still have unused reserves of fuels and ores.

The results of failure, however, would be so momentous from the point of view of man and the evolution of this part of the universe that it would seem wise to make the most pessimistic assumptions possible, and for man at this stage to make a concerted and deliberate effort to avoid the waste of his exhaustible resources in war and luxury and to concentrate their use in expanding knowledge in the direction of achieving a closed-cycle, high-level system. To some extent classical civilization, in so far as it is based on a permanent agriculture, represents a low-level or perhaps one should say a medium-level, closed-cycle economy, and we could presumably always retreat to this. Once the exhaustible resources are gone, however, it is very doubtful whether man could ever break out of this medium-level economy, and as far as he is concerned the evolutionary process would have come to an end. We cannot afford to take even a small chance of a failure which would have consequences for millions of years in the future.

Our chance of solving these problems depends mainly on the evolutionary potential which is present in the scientific method, as we saw in Chapter II. The scientific method is essentially an evolutionary mutation in man's means of acquiring knowledge. It is a mutation, furthermore, with enormous potential. This potential is probably not unlimited, and there will come a day when the full potential of the scientific method will be exhausted and all that man can know with this method will be known. This day, however, now seems a very long way off, and I should be very surprised to learn that we have exhausted more than a small fraction of this potential.

It may be, for instance, that many of the problems relating to energy and man's material environment will be solved in the course of the revolution in biological knowledge which is now under way and, indeed, still in a very early stage. We now seem to be at the point in biology which we reached in regard to nuclear energy about 1900. In 1900 we knew that nuclear energy existed but we could not conceive of any way of liberating it. At the present moment we know that the life is transmitted and organized through a "code" contained in a molecular structure of genes, but we know only the rudiments of the language of this code and we do not know how to "speak" it ourselves. That is, we cannot except in the most rudimentary way manipulate the genetic structure to create new forms of life. Once the basic knowledge has been found, however, its application seems to follow almost inevitably in the space of a generation or two.

It seems probable, therefore, that we are on the edge of biological revolution which may make both the wonders and horrors of nuclear revolution seem relatively insignificant by comparison.

It may therefore well be that the solution of the problem of a stable, closed-cycle, high-level technology will be found in the development of superior biological processes and artificial forms of life. The mechanics of life is much more refined and efficient in detail than the mechanics of non-living machines, and the manipulation of the mechanics of life would enormously increase human power. We may develop even in the next decade or so new races of one-celled organisms much more useful to man than the existing ones. Enormous increases in the food supply, coupled with the utilization of solar energy, may be possible through organisms of this kind. When we look a little further into the future it is at least not absurd to think of "super horses," of living tissue grafted into mechanical devices, of men with largely artificial and "improved" insides, and of computers made of brain tissue *in vitro*. We can think of machines as we know them today as very crude simulators of the machinery of life. The automobile, for instance, is a crude extension of man's mechanical body, and a visitor from outer space at this stage of world history might well conclude that we were developing a race of large four-wheeled bugs with detachable brains! We are caught in a process here which will raise very fundamental questions about the nature and destiny of man, about his ideals regarding his own person, and even about what might be his successor. Indeed the idea that man might create his successor is no longer so fanciful as it seemed even twenty-five years ago.

Beyond biology the development of the social sciences again offers some helpful solutions—or, at the most pessimistic, *some* help toward the solutions—of the more subtle problems of entropy and disorganization associated with man's own nature and his social organization. The crucial theoretical problem here is the understanding of the process of human learning. Here we do not yet seem to have reached the stage of theoretical breakthrough as we have in biology. What we know about human learning is fragmentary, and up to now, at any rate, has produced very little change and perhaps even no change for the better in the processes by which we acquire knowledge and values, and by which we test the reality of our images of the world around us, especially in regard to social systems. Once we are aware, however, that there is something that we do not know, there is a strong tendency for research to be directed toward it. The problem of human learning is fundamental to the solution of all social problems. It will be surprising if some major efforts are not directed toward it, and it will be also surprising if some fundamental theoretical discoveries are not made.

The increase in power over ourselves which will result from such discoveries would have enormous potentialities both for good and for evil. As suggested earlier, we might collapse into a world of meaningless hedonism. On the other hand one can visualize a world in which what passes for genius today becomes commonplace, and in which elements of human personality and capability which we now recognize as both superior and rare become widespread. It is obvious today that most people do not begin to approach their full capacity for knowledge or even for enjoyment of their own nervous system. An increase in the knowledge of man which would enable more people to live closer to their capacity seems like a reasonable end product of the present processes of scientific development. The pity and the tragedy of mankind is that he falls so far short of his capacity, and it surely is the major objective of the whole developmental process to enable man to realize the capacity with which he is endowed by his genetic equipment. We may even look beyond this point and see human knowledge applied to improving man's genetic equipment itself, though what this does to our unimproved descendants may perhaps be left to the writers of science fiction!

It is impossible to predict genuine mutations and inventions, because if we could predict them we would already have them. Nevertheless as we study the evolutionary process we see how future developments are in some sense foreshadowed in earlier forms. Many of the things which make us human are found even in an amoeba. The first vertebrate skeleton foreshadowed an enormous evolutionary potential, in liberating life from the confines of the exoskeleton. The cries of animals and the dances of the bee foreshadow language and perhaps even the bowerbird and the pack rat foreshadow art. The silent trade of the savage foreshadows the elaborate markets of today. In the primitive family we see the roots of a large number of social organizations.

Now if we look around us today to see what in man's experience looks like the foreshadowing of things to come, we may well find it in the experience of the mystics and the gropings of man in religion. It will be surprising indeed if man as we know him today represented the total exhaustion of all evolutionary potential. As our knowledge of reality grows so does our ignorance, and it will again be surprising if in this early stage of man's development he has exhausted all his modes of communication with reality. Even though, therefore, mechanism is the midwife of the great transition, the end results may well be a society specializing in spiritual experiences of a quality which we now realize only in rare moments of intuition.

VIII.

The Role of Ideology in the Great Transition

THE dynamics of society are governed by two sets of circumstances which the sociologist Robert Merton has called "latent" and "manifest." The latent forces are those of which we are not aware or only dimly aware, or in which awareness plays an unimportant role. The manifest processes are those in which the awareness of the process itself— that is, the image of the nature of society and the social processes in the minds of men—plays a significant role in determining the behavior of men and the course of social events.

In biological evolution almost the whole process is latent in this sense. The participants in the process are not themselves aware of what is going on, or even if they have some awareness, this plays no role in the process. An animal, for instance, may be aware of its immediate surroundings but

156

it has no knowledge even of its own life process and still less of the great evolutionary process of which it is a part. It is the peculiar glory of man that he has developed not only awareness of his immediate environment but awareness of much larger processes in which he plays a part. In so far as he develops this awareness the processes themselves are changed. The image of the world in the minds of men then becomes an essential element in the process of the world itself. As awareness develops it gradually penetrates all aspects of the system of the universe. The planets used to pursue their courses unaware and undisturbed by awareness. Now man has introduced new planets, however small, into the solar system and the solar system will never be the same again. Man has now created new elements, new sources of radiation, and his prying fingers are now actively turning the key of life itself, so that awareness is beginning to enter the very process of biological evolution.

Into man's social systems awareness has entered from the very first, even though in early days it took primitive and often mistaken forms. It is this element of awareness of the social system itself which differentiates the social systems of man from those of the mammals or the insects. The ants and the bees have elaborate social systems or things that have the outward appearance of social systems. These do not, however, have the property of self-awareness of the nature of the social system itself; hence they are quite different in quality from the social systems of man. A beehive or an anthill indeed can more properly be regarded as a super-organism than as a social system. The individual bee or ant is more like an organ in an organism than it is like a person in society. Because of this the social systems of ants and bees are essentially static in nature and do not exhibit adaptation to the environment beyond what biological mutation can provide. With man, however, comes self-awareness, and not only self-awareness but awareness of a whole system in which the self in embedded. This can produce conscious effort toward a change in the system of the world whether biological, physical, or social. In any human social system, therefore, the image of the world possessed by its human participants is a vital element in the over-all dynamics of the system. We cannot tell what the system will do unless we know what the people in it think of it, for what they think affects their behavior and their behavior affects the system.

What they think need not of course be true. We have already looked at some of the problems involved in the concept of the truth of an image, and we need not go into these philosophical difficulties again. It is sufficient to note that the presence of any image will affect a system in a certain way. Some images move the system in directions which are better in terms of its own values and some in directions which are worse. The thing which can be tested, oddly enough, is not the truth of an image but its goodness, either in terms of its own value system or in terms of some other value system which we impose on it. The really tricky problem here is how changes in value systems occur, as indeed they do all the time. For the moment I think we must simply accept this fact without understanding it very well.

An ideology may be defined as that part of his image of the world which a person defines as essential to his identity or his image of himself. The greater part of our image of the world is not usually part of an ideology. We have in our minds, for instance, an image of the city in which we live as a "map" of streets, bus lines, and so on, which enables us to find our way about in it. This image of space, however, is not very important in creating our personal identity even though the place where we live is certainly a part of our identity. But when a person says, "I am a Communist," or, "I am a Buddhist," or, "I am an American," a whole set of images of the world is implied in the statement which are closely bound up with the personal identity of the individual. His ideology, therefore, is a part of a man's image of the world which is peculiarly valuable to him and which he is concerned to defend and propagate. In many people, perhaps in most people, the ideological component of the image is weak or even nonexistent. Such people build their identities around a few personal relationships in the family or the neighborhood or around their occupational identity. If you ask a man what he "is" and he says "a farmer" or if a woman says "just a housewife," the inference is that the ideological component is weak. As we get nearer to positions of power, however, especially political or ecclesiastical power, the ideological component is likely to be stronger, and for this reason if for no other the ideological tides which have swept across the face of history have had profound consequences for mankind. The history of social systems indeed is largely written in terms of these ideological tides, Buddhism, Christianity, Islam, Communism, and various nationalisms and imperialisms that have swept over parts of the world from time to time, have retreated and advanced, and have profoundly affected the lives of men.

At some periods of history, ideologies have exhibited sharp geographical boundaries and have been dominant in certain areas and almost absent outside them. When this has been the case the competition among ideologies has almost invariably been dangerous and costly, for the commonest way to change a boundary is through war. By contrast, in periods when ideologies have been geographically diffused so that their adherents were geographically intermingled, toleration has generally been forced on them by the sheer fact of physical coexistence, and the conflict among them has been relatively mild. A good example of this proposition can be seen in the conflict between Catholicism and Protestantism. In the fifteenth to sixteenth centuries, when these ideologies were associated with particular nations and states, the conflict between them was costly and bloody indeed. After the peace of Westphalia in 1648 a pattern of coexistence gradually developed until now these ideologies engage mainly in peaceful competition, even though there are some states predominantly Catholic and others predominantly Protestant. In many countries Protestants and Catholics mix in the same society and there are no sharp geographical boundaries which divide them.

We can see immediately that the sharp geographical separation between the Communist world or the socialist camp, as the Communists call it themselves, and the self-styled free world presents a grave danger under the present circumstances. Each ideology becomes highly intolerant of the other, and the adherents of each ideology form an alienated minority on one side of the boundary and the dominant power on the other. The danger that ideological conflict may degenerate into war under these circumstances is very great, and as we have seen, war presents the most immediate threat to the achievement of the great transition. Anything which therefore can mitigate or moderate ideological conflict in the present circumstances is so much gain, and anything which intensifies it is a threat to man's future. Therefore an understanding of ideologies, of man's need for them, and of the circumstances under which they can be modified is a crucial component in the achievement of the great transition.

What is it, then, that gives to an image of the world power over a man's mind and that leads him to build his personal identity around it? The answer seems to be that an image of the world becomes an ideology if it creates in the mind of the person holding it a role for himself which he values highly. New ideologies are therefore likely to arise if people feel that the roles which they occupy in the existing society are unsatisfactory to them or despised by others. To create a role, however, an ideology must create a drama. The first essential characteristic of an ideology is then an interpretation of history sufficiently dramatic and convincing so that the individual feels that he can identify with it and which in turn can give the individual a role in the drama it portrays.

Thus Christianity portrays history as a grand drama of the salvation of man by the intervention of God in Christ. The individual by becoming a Christian identifies with this drama and accepts a role in it. Communism likewise portrays history as a great drama of class struggle in which the ultimate triumph of the proletariat will see the end of this process and the establishment of justice upon earth. In becoming a Communist an individual likewise sees himself as performing a role in a drama of large dimensions. It is indeed a smaller scale version of the cosmic drama of the Christian faith.

Going along with an interpretation of history is usually some view of the nature of reality and the sources of knowledge from which the interpretation of history is derived. Furthermore if the individual is to play a role, there must be a value system capable of developing principles of moral action and a standard for the criticism of behavior. The individual must be able to judge when he is performing the role well and when he is performing it badly. An interpretation of history applied to social systems also implies a value system applied to political behavior and decisions. The possessor of an ideology eats of the fruit of the tree of knowledge and is thereby able to distinguish good from evil; he knows who is a bad guy and who is a good guy, and, of course, he is allied with the good guys! Every ideology must have all these elements present to some degree, though there are some ideologies which lay more stress on the interpretation of history and others which lay more stress on the personal role.

An ideology is therefore likely to be a syndrome in the image of the world, if one may borrow a term from medicine. A syndrome is a set of reinforcing symptoms and conditions all of which tend to go together. Similarly in an ideology each part will reinforce the other with an internal logic and consistency. This has a powerful effect in reinforcing belief, for as an individual thinks of one part of ideology his belief in other parts is reinforced. Thus an ideology which states that the world is essentially meaningless but that we ought to strive, suffer, and fight for it is unlikely to be powerful because of the essential contradiction among its components. If an interpretation of history says the world is meaningless, then our value system is likely to be pure hedonism—"Eat, drink, and be merry, for tomorrow we die"—or else one of apathy or stoic resignation.

An ideology by contrast which has a clear image of a significant and exciting future and a clear view of what people have to do in order to achieve this future is likely to be powerful whether or not it is true. There is a great deal indeed in the suggestion made by Fred Polak* that the ability of an ideology to organize society depends in large measure on the optimistic or pessimistic quality of its images of the future and on whether it holds that the future can be changed by human activity.

On the other hand if an image of the world is too rational and too consistent it does not become an ideology simply because it does not differentiate the identity of the person holding it from that of anybody else. It would be hard to build an ideology around the multiplication table, for nobody would be against it. Images of the world involving truths which are obvious to all do not become ideologies. It is the half truth, or at least the insecure truth, which appeals to some but not to others, which is the best candidate to set up an ideology. It is frequently the symbols toward which we are ambivalent that have the greatest power over us. The obviously bad we simply reject. The obviously good we simply accept. But it is the things which attract and repel us at the same time that hold us as it were in a bind. The power of Communism among its followers, for instance, arises in part because it combines on the one hand a lofty idealism and a genuine concern for the welfare of mankind, along with the most unprincipled deceit, chicanery, violence, and coercion. The appeal of nationalism likewise rests on a similar ambivalence. The nation is at the same time the protector of widows and the roaster of chil-

* Fred Polak, *The Image of the Future,* New York, Oceana Press, 1960.

dren—social security and Hiroshima combined in a single body.

An important element in the dynamics of ideological interaction is the ability of an ideology to change without collapsing. Ideologies are always under pressure of some kind, if only because of the contradictions and ambivalences which seem necessarily connected with them. If, for instance, the expectations which it produces are persistently disappointed, the truth of the ideology will be suspect, and once this happens the power of the ideology is bound to wane. It has been said indeed, rather cynically, that an ideology goes through three stages. At first people believe in it, then they believe in believing in it, and then they cease to believe in it. The second stage, however, can last a long time. An ideology which has been successful in organizing a society, and which is associated in the minds of its adherents with persons or events which they admire for reasons quite unconnected with the ideology, may have a long life in the second stage even though the original fire may have gone out of it. There is evidence, for instance, that Communism in Russia has already reached this stage whereas in China it has certainly not.

Sometimes ideologies collapse dramatically. The British imperial ideology, for instance, as represented by Rudyard Kipling, collapsed dramatically between 1910 and 1920—perhaps as a result of the First World War. The *laissez faire* ideology in the United States suffered a certain collapse as a result of the great depression of 1929–33. On the other hand the change of an ideology is not the same thing as the collapse of a society or even of the death of the organization embodied in it. The ideology of both nations and churches change continually, but the organizations continue. This can happen under a legitimate and necessary process of reality testing.

Ideologies in society can also change slowly without collapse and without destructive conflicts. This might be called the process of the dialogue as opposed to the dialectic. In a dialogue or a conversation the image of each participant is continually modified in response to information received from the other. Nobody "wins" a conversation and yet the images of the world may be profoundly modified in it. Therefore the more we can establish dialogue among ideologies the less dangerous the ideological conflict becomes, and the more likely is it to be fruitful and to develop into a true learning process.

The danger of ideology is that it suppresses the learning process. If a man has an ideology which explains everything that happens to him, it relieves him of the necessity for learning. He knows everything already! The great dilemma of ideology therefore is that while it is capable of resolving internal conflict both in the individual and in the society and therefore of generating substantial power and motive force, in the course of generating this powerful engine it is likely to destroy the steering wheel and the compass. That is, it injures the learning process and the process of reality testing which are the only true guides to the *direction* of development. The ideal of course is to combine the powerful engine with the sensitive compass, and develop an image of the world which can provide motivation without impairing the capacity for learning about what is the best direction of change.

With these considerations in mind let us then turn to the ideological struggle of the present day, that between the socialist camp led by the Soviet Union and the market economies led by the United States. Even within these two camps there is of course a great variety of ideological belief and expression. This variety has increased in recent years, especially within the socialist camp, but still there is a great gulf even between the socialist capitalism of Scandinavia and the capitalist socialism of Yugoslavia.

The ideological rift is deep and real, producing societies which are very different in style, flavor, and quality of human life. In the socialist camp, ideology is more clearly formulated and is more an official part of the society. Ideology in the West is vaguer and much more diffused. In this respect the West is "Protestant" whereas the East is "Catholic." From the point of view of the impact of ideology on individual life, the Soviet Union is much more like Spain than it is like the United States. On the other hand, in terms of the practical disposition of its resources and the general character of its people, the Soviet Union is more like the United States than it is like Spain, simply because it is further along toward the great transition.

In view of the immense literature on the subject, it seems

presumptuous to attempt to summarize the differences between the two ideologies in a few paragraphs. The essential differences, however, seem to me relatively simple. We shall find indeed that at the level of ultimate values and objectives the two ideologies are much more similar than appears at first sight. The differences arise mainly because of differences in the image of society and social causation, and differences in the assessment of certain instrumental values and institutional arrangements. As we noticed earlier, either ideological disagreements can be at the level of basic values, in which case they are extremely difficult to resolve, or they can be at the level of instrumental values—that is, things which are valued because they are believed to be necessary in order to achieve the basic values. In this latter case the dispute should be much more amenable to scientific testing.

One basic value common to both East and West today might be described as disalienation—that is, the development of a society from which no one will feel or be excluded or alien and in which all will have equal rights and equal privileges, in one at least of the many senses of the word equality. It is only in the backwaters of Western society such as South Africa, Alabama, or Portugal that one finds today any conscious defenders of a society of immobile castes and class stratification. The ethical principle which is at the base of much socialist ideology and which gives it much of its power might be called familism: the idea that all members of society and ultimately all members of the human race are part of a single family and therefore each has responsibility for all. However, this is neither more nor less than the idea of the brotherhood of man long preached and little practiced by all the great world religions. It is a vital part of whatever passes for ideology in the West as well as in the East.

At the instrumental level, however, the ideologies then proceed to divide. The Communist regards the class struggle as the key to history, culminating in the final triumph of the proletariat and the establishment of the classless society under the leadership of an elite and socially aware party. For the Communist it is the private ownership of the means of production which creates the fundamental alienation of the proletariat from the society which is run by the propertied and for the propertied. The only remedy in their eye, therefore, is violent revolution in which the propertied classes are dispossessed and the state as the representative of whole society takes over the ownership and administration of the means of production.

Fitting closely into this interpretation of history is an instrumental ethic which denies all legitimacy to private property, private profit, and the private ownership of capital, an ethic which is given a pseudoscientific sanction by Karl Marx's theory of surplus value. By denying the legitimacy of private profit the socialists largely cut themselves off from the possibility of organizing society through the institution of the market. They are forced then to organize the society through the institution of the national budget or plan. The socialist society then becomes a one-firm state in which the control of all economic activity is concentrated in a single massive organization.

This ideology seems to have very little appeal in the developed countries of the West, where it is confined for the most part to rather small sectarian groups. As development proceeds, the class structure of a society becomes more complex, and the Marxian prediction that the rich will get richer and the poor poorer has been completely falsified. The ownership of property in such a society becomes very widespread even though the bulk of ownership is still concentrated in about 10 per cent of the population. Under these circumstances the class war in Marx's sense becomes rather meaningless, and the political conflicts in society tend to be between occupational or regional groups rather than between classes. The working class indeed becomes a fiction which has no reality either in a common sentiment or common organization. The working class is fragmented into innumerable regional and occupational groups, and national consciousness becomes much stronger than class consciousness. The movement toward the classless society or at least toward the integrated society then takes place not through revolution, or indeed through any dialectical process, but through a process of political dialogue, compromise, and the sheer working out of the social consequences of a long-continued process of economic growth. In the developed capitalist countries a true proletariat still exists, but it has become a minority, and furthermore, unfortunately, an impotent minority.

Under these circumstances Marx's interpretation of history simply ceases to have much meaning, and the attempt to force history into a dialectical form results merely in hairsplitting and intellectual dishonesty. The Communist party discredits itself simply because it does not speak to the needs of the society around it. It is working with a model of society which may be applicable in some times and places but which is by no means universal, and which is particularly inapplicable to the circumstances of a society enjoying rapid development under the market institutions.

Just as the class struggle and the dialectical interpretation of history evoke little response in a society which is obviously going another way, so the theory of surplus value and the attack on profit as such, or on private ownership in the means of production as such, fall on deaf ears. The organized working class perceives that its main line of advancement is through the exercise of market power. This is the essence of what is called business unionism. The industrial worker indeed, who was seen by Marx as the man of the future, rapidly becomes the man of the past. Every increase in technological efficiency reduces the proportion of population in this category and increases the proportion in professional, managerial, and service occupations. The industrial worker therefore gets too rich and too scarce to function as the Marxian proletariat, and has very little incentive or

opportunity to foment a revolution. If, however, he perceives his main avenue to advancement as a rise in wages,
he becomes committed to the market system, and the market
system is unworkable without private property and private
profit. The labor movement therefore becomes a conserva-
tive force and a strong defender of the market economy,
even to the extent of supporting the basic institutions of
capitalism.

Under the circumstances where the market economy is
obviously providing constantly increasing real income for
all, the "one firm state" of the socialist then looks like a
monstrous concentration of economic and political power
designed mainly to exploit the working class in the interest
of the power of the state itself, and completely defenseless
against capture by ruthless dictators. Marx's description of
the state as a committee of the bourgeoisie seems fan-
tastically inappropriate to, say, the American federal government as we know it in the twentieth century. Popular
nationalism indeed has turned out to be a far more powerful integrating force in society than either the unity of the
working class under socialism (or for that matter Christianity or any other religion) as indeed the current split
between Russia and China demonstrates. The Soviet Union
was simply not prepared to sacrifice its own development
for the sake of assisting Chinese development. The unity of
the working class is clearly a myth, even within the socialist
camp. Had it really existed the Soviet Union would have
made massive sacrifices in order to assist the Chinese in

their development. As it was, all the Soviet Union did for China was to grant a loan—at interest—amounting to about ten cents per Chinese per year, and to send a few technicians who were suddenly withdrawn with disastrous consequences in 1960. The Russians are Russians and the Chinese are Chinese long before they are either proletarian or socialist. The gap between the rich countries and the poor is much wider and more important than any gap between the rich and the poor within any one country, especially within any one developed country.

The successes of Communism are due to an aspect of its ideology which is quite separable from the foregoing. This is its explicit recognition of the nature of economic development and its self-conscious orientation toward it. The great transition in the West has taken place as a result largely of ecological forces, and without much conscious planning until recently. The Industrial Revolution in England certainly began and got under way not as a result of any conscious efforts on the part of the government or even of any individual who participated in it, but because of the interaction of individual decisions and certain latent forces in the society.

Following the publication of the *Wealth of Nations* by Adam Smith in 1776 the Western European countries and especially the United States became more self-conscious about the process of economic development, and indeed from that point on the development of these countries is much less accidental than it might look at first sight. The development of the United States especially was guided throughout by a policy which was quite self-conscious in its emphasis on the role of the market mechanism and also was not adverse to interfering with that mechanism by protective tariffs in the supposed interest of economic development. Nevertheless it is fair to say that the Communists have been more self-conscious about economic development than the countries of the West, and that the success of Communism where it has been successful is mainly a result of the willingness of these societies to put large amounts of resources into the growth industries, especially into education and capital goods. This has often been done inefficiently, and with great human cost, mainly because of the prejudice which these societies have against the market mechanism. If a society puts a lot of resources into growth, however, even though it does this very inefficiently, it is bound to grow.

The point at issue here is whether the market mechanism or the budget mechanism is the more developed form of social organization, and this seems to be a clear case in which dialogue is much more fruitful than a dialectical confrontation. The ideological crystallization into the two camps tends to prevent rational discussion of this problem on both sides in terms of the real issue—which is that of the optimum mix of the market and budget mechanism in any particular society. The extreme positions on both sides seem to be untenable. The claim of the extreme advocates of *laissez faire* that the market mechanism is sufficient to do all the jobs required of society has been clearly discredited by many occasions on which the market machinery has proved inadequate. There are some wants, like that for sexual satisfaction, in which the market machinery is regarded as illegitimate; there are public goods for the provision of which the market machinery is inappropriate; and there is a basic necessity in society for supervising the market machinery to see that it does not get out of hand and give us depressions, inflations, or unacceptable distributions of income. Furthermore the demands of familistic ethics even in a market society require the existence of a grants economy to provide for both people and functions for which the market does not make adequate provision.

On the other hand the socialist economies are severely handicapped by their refusal to make rational use of the price system and of private property and private profit. The grudging acceptance of these institutions at the margins of a society, for instance in the New Economic Policy of the 1920's, or in the peasant plots and city markets of the later periods, unquestionably contributed to the survival of the Soviet society, but the prejudices of the ideology prohibit any rational examination of the proper social role of free markets. In what might be called the halfhearted socialist societies like Ceylon, Burma, and Indonesia, the "mix" seems to be almost the worst possible, combining the socialist disorganization of the market economy with *laissez faire* in the matter of allocating resources to growth!

In the light of the great transition the whole ideological

struggle between capitalism and socialism takes on a certain air of irrelevance. It is clear by this time that development can take place under socialism. It is equally clear that it can also take place under capitalism, and that if it does take place successfully under capitalism, socialism becomes largely irrelevant to these societies at least in the sense of totalitarian socialism as we know it in the Communist countries. I have expressed this in what I call the doctrine of the missed bus. The bus for socialism comes along only at one stage of economic development. This is the early stage of capitalist development, when there is still a large proletarian working class, when there are still large inequalities of income, when development perhaps is concentrated in certain cities or areas of the society so that sharp disparities of income appear between the developed sectors and the undeveloped sectors, and when there are enough remains of feudal institutions and attitudes around to make the concept of class structure and class war look fairly realistic. Under these circumstances the Marxist ideology has a considerable appeal, and if this appeal has been heard by a small group of intellectuals who form a party, then especially if there is some internal upheaval such as a war or a spontaneous revolution, the party can capture the revolution, push the society into the socialist bus, and off it goes. Once in the socialist bus it is pretty hard for the society to get off it, and its development will follow a rather different path from then on.

If, however, the society misses the bus for one reason or

another, either because a revolutionary situation never develops, or because it develops before the self-conscious party has developed, and if then the society enjoys a successful process of capitalist or market development, the socialist bus never comes by again, and the socialist solution becomes less and less relevant. In the Western European countries 1848 may well have been the moment at which, if there had been a Communist party, it might have taken over. This, however, was too early. The Communist Manifesto was not enough to create a party. This had to wait for *Das Kapital* and almost two generations of socialist atheologians. In the United States it is doubtful whether the bus ever came by at all. There was that moment in 1932 when it might almost have been seen far down the street. Even then, at the height of depression, the Communists never became more than a modest threat. They failed to capture the imagination of the Negroes, with whom some success might have been expected, and their behavior gradually discredited them in the labor movement, from which they have been eventually expelled.

The ideological struggle is so dangerous today mainly because a large part of the world is still at the stage where the socialist bus has not yet come along, and the question is therefore open as to whether these societies will proceed in their development along totalitarian socialist lines or along the lines of what might be called the guided market economy. If the choice is between totalitarian socialist development and development under a successfully guided

market economy the answer would be pretty clear. Totalitarian socialist development is a very high-cost form. It has
a high cost in terms of refugees, in terms of terror and
violence, in terms of propaganda, manipulation, lies, and
the corruption of artistic and intellectual life. A non-
totalitarian socialist development is not inconceivable. The
closest approximation of this is unquestionably Poland,
where a great deal of intellectual and artistic liberty coexists
with socialist planning. Up to now, however, the brute fact
is that almost all socialist development has been totalitarian
and has been made at a very high cost in human suffering
and human corruption.

We must not blind ourselves, however, to the fact that
all development has a cost, and that unsuccessful capitalist
development of the sort that can be seen in Africa, Asia,
or some Latin American countries likewise has a high
human cost—as high as, if not higher than, the human cost
of totalitarian socialism. On the whole I am inclined to
think of these cases as totalitarian capitalist development,
and all the evidence points to the fact that it is the totalitarian element in the society, the reliance on the short cut
of violence and coercion, which leads to the high cost. The
sensible thing to look for, however, is development at least
cost, and what the least cost is in any society is likely to be a
function of its previous institutions. We cannot lay down
any hard and fast rules as to what the mix should be
between market and budget elements. I am inclined to the
paradox that a society in which the noneconomic elements

in life have a strong familistic or socialist character the institutions of capitalism and the market economy will work very well because they are constantly guided and checked by the "socialist" ethic. I would cite the United States as a good case in point. On the other hand in societies where the sense of community is weak and where the sense of the responsibility of each for all is poorly developed, the institutions of capitalism can be quite corrupting. China before the revolution may well be an example. If we are to achieve a least-cost transition we must stop dichotomizing the world and develop a pragmatic, indeed a social scientific approach to the problem.

Therefore, if there is any ideology peculiarly appropriate to the achievement of the transition it is neither capitalism nor socialism but the scientific ideology itself applied to society. An ideology for the great transition must then be a strategy rather than an ideology. This I will endeavor to formulate in the next chapter.

IX.

A Strategy for the Transition

THE fact of the great transition is not in dispute. Almost anyone in middle life today has simply to look back to his own childhood, or still more to the days of his grandparents, to realize that we are living in a world in which there is an enormous rate of change. If anyone in an advanced society today were to be suddenly thrust back into the world of only a hundred years ago, he would feel utterly alien and strange. A considerable part of his vocabulary would be meaningless to the people around him. He would find it hard to adapt to the inconveniences and to the restricted life which he would have to lead. He would feel indeed in an alien society.

It is the business of this final chapter to look at the attitudes which may be taken toward the transition and to outline the possible strategy for achieving the transition at the least cost in terms of human misery and degradation. Attitudes toward the transition can range from rejection, through a grudging acceptance, to a cautious and critical acceptance, and to an enthusiastic and uncritical acceptance. It will become clear, I think, that I take my own stand somewhere about the third of these positions. I welcome the transition as an event of enormous evolutionary potential, in line with the general development of the universe as we know it. On the other hand, it has great potential for evil as well as for good, and the transition itself involves the human race in dangers which are so great as to be almost unacceptable. All four attitudes outlined above should therefore be examined and none should be rejected out of hand.

It is frequently possible for a form of life or a form of society to reject a new evolutionary step. Indeed, to some extent this seems to be necessary. The world as we know it today contains innumerable examples of surviving forms and species which represent earlier stages of evolutionary development. Plenty of hydrogen, which may have been the first element to evolve, is still around. Inorganic material still dominates the universe in a quantitative sense. The virus, the amoeba, and a very large number of examples of lower forms of life are still with us. Paleolithic and neolithic man still survives in remote corners of the world. It is therefore reasonable to suppose that civilized society could coexist for a very long time with postcivilized society and that this might happen not only because of an inability to make the transition but because of an unwillingness to make it. Even within an advanced society like the United States there are small groups like the Amish who preserve an eighteenth-century culture. Spain and Portugal deliberately rejected modernization in the interest of a "civilized" value system which they believe to be superior to anything which an advanced society can offer. In a different context, Thailand and Burma seem to have made the same choice. India is profoundly unwilling to give up certain aspects of her ancient civilized culture which are inconsistent with economic development. It may well be, therefore, that the option of rejecting the great transition is open to many societies and that the choice can deliberately be made one way or the other. In the light of a long historical perspective, we may even see the socialist countries become fixated on a nineteenth-century social science and world view, so that they will therefore proceed through the transition only up to some halfway point. We cannot be sure of this, but it is at least something for the socialist society to worry about!

What we do not know are the exact conditions under which the option to reject the great transition and remain in the state of civilization is really open. The amoeba remains with us, after hundreds of millions of years of evolution, but innumerable older forms of life have not survived. Sometimes the choice between participating in an evolutionary development or not participating in it is not open. Those forms which do not participate in the development do not survive. This process is as evident in social evolution as it is in biological evolution. If indeed a successful new development is to be rejected, the species or the society which rejects the development must have some kind of niche in the system of ecological equilibrium which includes the developed species. Either this niche must be the result of geographical isolation, such as that which permitted the survival of marsupials and even paleolithic man in Australia, or the older species must be able to find a place in the social or ecological equilibrium which will enable it to reproduce sufficiently for survival. This may require some adaptation on its part.

The isolation of a relatively small subculture in a modern world is possible, even though it may be difficult, as the examples of the Amish in the United States and the Baptists and Old Believers in the Soviet Union demonstrate. Similarly national societies which reject the great transition, or which find themselves incapable of achieving it, may likewise survive even in a postcivilized world as long as they are neither a threat nor a temptation to the more developed societies around them. Furthermore, in a world in which there is a deadly fear of war, and fear, moreover, that even small wars may escalate into big ones, there will be a strong tendency to freeze existing national boundaries; and hence nations which are only conditionally viable in the military sense may remain undisturbed for a long period of time.

Nevertheless there are strong arguments on the other side, and it may well be that for many societies the choice between civilization and postcivilization is not really open. The choice which *is* open may be a more grim one, between a painful and difficult advance into postcivilization and an agonizing retreat into anarchy and numbing poverty. We have seen many instances in history of the impact of civilized on precivilized societies which has been in almost every case disastrous for the precivilized society unless it has been able to achieve a successful reorganization. That is, when civilization hits a precivilized society it cannot remain as it was. Either it must make an adjustment to civilization or it will disintegrate. The Plains Indians in the United States are an example of a total failure to adjust with consequent disintegration of the old society. Some of the Indians of the Southwest, such as the Hopi, represent cases of partial adjustment. Hawaii perhaps represents the case of total adjustment and absorption into advanced culture, with very little of the old society left. The cargo cults of Melanesia likewise represent the disintegration of an old precivilized society under contact with "civilization" in the Second World War, even civilization in its less agreeable aspects.

On the other hand there have also been many examples in which precivilized or barbarian societies have overthrown civilizations. The tale of the destruction of cities and civilizations by barbarian invaders is an old one and a long one. It is not, however, the truly precivilized societies which overthrow civilization but what might be called semicivilized societies which have acquired enough of the arts of civilization to advance their destructive power, but not enough to be constructive. One can therefore see that just as the interaction of civilized with precivilized societies carries great dangers to both of them and often indeed destroys both, so the interaction of postcivilized and civilized societies involves great dangers, dangers indeed which are intensified by the increased powers of destruction involved in postcivilized techniques. /On the one side, as we have already seen, the introduction of public health measures into civilized societies almost inevitably involves them in disastrous population explosions if radical changes in the pattern of culture do not follow very rapidly. Indeed the probability is deplorably high that many of these societies in the next fifty years will sink into hopeless apathy or even into anarchy as the result of their failure to make the necessary demographic adjustments. On the other hand the nightmare of a new Tamerlane or Genghis Khan equipped with nuclear weapons also must be faced. Even if the developed countries of the world achieve a condition of peaceful coexistence, as seems not impossible, the pattern of previous history would seem to suggest a possibility of a ruthless conqueror arising in a less developed country—some Macedonia or Mongolia of the twenty-first century possessed of nuclear or biological weapons but not of the basic culture which produces them—who might then unleash a new fury of a destruction against the postcivilized world.

The conclusion of all this argument is that the rejection of postcivilization is possible only under limited circumstances and that this rejection cannot be a simple rejection of the kind which refuses to make any adjustment but must in itself be a conscious adjustment to the new world situation. Even so, this option is not likely to be open to everybody. In the course of development there is a point of no return, after which the option of remaining merely civilized is no longer available. The society is caught up in a dynamic of change which no power can stop. This, indeed, is the significance of Rostow's* concept of the "take-off." There are also societies which are so placed geographically that they cannot remain isolated. One wonders indeed whether in an age of air transportation and intercontinental missiles any society now has the option which was clearly open to Tokugawa Japan in the seventeenth century. Japan could isolate itself from the processes of development, at least from external pressure, because it was geographically remote from the centers in Europe where postcivilization first got under way. This remoteness, however, ended by the middle of the nineteenth century, even before the age of air travel, and Japan made the choice for development. Japan decided in effect that it could not survive as a "merely" civilized country. But remoteness has utterly disappeared from the earth, and it seems probable that a "Tokugawa solution" is no longer available for any country, unless "social" distance can be established through the development of a framework of world security.

An attitude of outright rejection of the great transition is rare. What is much more common is an attitude of grudging acceptance. This, however, may be even more disastrous than an attitude of outright rejection, for it usually involves wanting the fruits of development without

* Walt W. Rostow, *The Stages of Economic Growth*, Cambridge University Press, 1960.

being prepared to incur the costs. The relative failure of development today in the tropical belt is perhaps more the result of the grudging and halfhearted acceptance of the idea of development than it is the result of any other single factor. Under these circumstances the probability may be tragically high that many of these societies will fail to make the adjustment and hence will actually go downhill in the next decades. There is a world of difference between poverty and destitution—between, say, the poverty of Jamaica and the destitution of Haiti, the poverty of Malaya and the destitution of parts of India. There is real danger that under the impact of isolation, population explosion, and political incompetence, many countries which are now poor will become destitute and under this condition may be desperately hard to change. Therefore of all the attitudes toward the great transition a grudging and therefore probably unsuccessful acceptance of the idea which implies a failure to realize it is the most disastrous.

Going now to the other extreme, we see in some cases an uncritical acceptance of any and all change provided that it has the appearance of being technological, progressive, or advanced. This attitude is particularly prevalent among the Communists, but it is by no means unknown in the West. It is probably not so dangerous an attitude as grudging acceptance or rejection, in the sense that it is less likely to lead to absolute failure or disaster, but it nevertheless is an attitude which has its own peculiar dangers, particularly when it is accompanied by a rigid ideological view on how the transition is to be achieved. Under these circumstances an attitude of this kind can easily result in what I call high-cost development. It may indeed be argued that high-cost development is better than no development at all and certainly better than development in the wrong direction. Still, it is clearly worse than low-cost development and it therefore needs to come under highly critical scrutiny. Where development has been attained at a higher cost than necessary—that is to say, in terms of human misery or degradation, social disorganization, and the loss of cherished values—this can usually be attributed either to a failure of organization or to failure of decision making because of false images of the social system. In the West, for instance, the transition has been accompanied by a good deal of potentially avoidable human misery in depressions and unemployment. There have often been inadequate provisions for education, old age, sickness, and an inadequate provision of those social goods which cannot be provided through markets. These costs may be attributed partly to a lack of political organization, partly to lags in the transfer of political power to a wider base, and most of all perhaps to an inadequate conscious image of the nature of the process through which the society was passing, with consequent political decisions based not only on an inadequate information system but also on an inadequate theoretical framework. Nevertheless the enthusiasm for development in the West and the willingness of its culture to absorb new products, new techniques, and new ideas has enabled it to overcome many of these difficulties; and though many of the costs have been high the returns have unquestionably exceeded the costs. If we were to do it again, we no doubt could do it better, but in a sense it is a miracle to have done it at all.

Likewise in the socialist countries there has been a very high-cost development, a cost which in my personal view exceeds even the high cost of the Western development in its early stages. For instance, the first collectivization of agriculture in the Soviet Union from 1928 to 1932 was a larger human disaster than the great depression in the West, almost by an order of magnitude. In the West there was massive unemployment, net investment declined almost to zero, poverty increased, and the process of development was interrupted though probably not reversed. The rate of development slowed down almost to zero but did not become negative. In the Soviet Union some six million people died, mainly of starvation, half the livestock was killed, a deliberately fanned class hatred disrupted the society, personal liberty was destroyed, and the arts stagnated. Out of this, it is true, emerged the heavy industry and the educational investment on which future growth could be built, and the Soviet citizens could well argue that the return has been greater than the cost. Nevertheless the cost was enormous and much of it was avoidable. Likewise in Communist China the costs of development are enormous, so high indeed that they may threaten the whole process and result in a desperately paranoid nation. Even in Cuba we see an enormously high-cost development with a cost in terms of refugees, the militarization and dehumanization of the society, and economic failures which again could easily have been avoided if the revolution had not fallen into the hands of those guided by an obsolete ideology. On the other hand in Yugoslavia, in Poland, and perhaps in Rumania and Bulgaria we see processes of socialist development at much less cost, even though here one would like to see the cost lowered even further, especially the cost in terms of personal liberty.

It is clear that the distinction between high-cost and low-cost development is something which cuts right across the cold war and the division of the world into East and West. I must confess that I think the socialist doctrine itself imposes a certain limit below which the cost of development cannot be reduced, but this limit may be tolerable and the costs of the least-cost socialist development may be much less than that of the high-cost capitalist development. When for instance we look at countries like Brazil, where development has been achieved at the high social cost of inflation, failure to provide social goods, and a certain moral disintegration of the society, and even more when we look at the many countries in the so-called free world where development has been unsuccessful, it is clear that we all live in glass houses and that no one can afford to throw stones. We all face the problem of developing realistic images of the dynamics of our particular social systems. In this task a dialogue between East and West may be of considerable value, but a dialectical confrontation is of little use. Still more, the passion, hatred, and propaganda which arise out of the cold war are no help at all.

I therefore have no hesitation in recommending the attitude toward the great transition which I have described as critical acceptance. There may be times when we wish nostalgically that it had never started, for then at least the danger that the evolutionary experiment in this part of the universe would be terminated would be more remote. Now that the transition is under way, however, there is no going back on it. We must learn to use its enormous potential for good rather than for evil, and we must learn to diminish and eventually eliminate the dangers which are inherent in it. If I had to sum up the situation in a sentence I would say that the situation has arisen because of the development of certain methods of reality testing applied to our images of nature. If we are to ride out the transition successfully we must apply these or similar methods for reality testing to our images of man and his society.

There is in the world today an "invisible college" of people in many different countries and many different cultures, who have this vision of the nature of the transition through which we are passing and who are determined to devote their lives to contributing toward its successful fulfillment. Membership in this college is consistent with many different philosophical, religious, and political positions. It is a college without a founder and without a president, without buildings and without organization. Its founding members might have included a Jesuit like Pierre Teilhard de Chardin, a humanist like Aldous Huxley, a writer of science fiction like H. G. Wells, and it might even have given honorary degrees to Adam Smith, Karl Marx, Pope John XXIII, and even Khrushchev and John F. Kennedy. Its living representatives are still a pretty small group of people. I think, however, that it is they who hold the future of the world in their hands or at least in their minds.

For this invisible college I am an unashamed propagandist and I confess without a blush that this book is a tract. Our precious little planet, this blue-green cradle of life with its rosy mantle, is in one of the most critical stages, perhaps the most critical stage, of its whole existence. It is in a position of immense danger and immense potentiality. There are no doubt many experiments in evolution going on in different parts of this big universe. But this happens to be my planet and I am very much attached to it, and I am desperately anxious that this particular experiment should be a success. If this be ethnocentrism, then let me be ethnocentric! I am pretty sure, however, that it will not be a success unless something is done. There is danger both of the bang of nuclear detonation and of the whimper of exhausted overpopulation, and either would mean an end of the evolutionary process in these parts. If man were merely capable of destroying himself, one could perhaps bear the thought. One could at least console oneself with the thought of elementary justice, that if man does destroy himself it is his own silly fault. He is captain, however, of a frail and delicate vessel, and in the course of destroying himself he might easily destroy the vessel—that is, the planet which carries him, with its immense wealth and variety of evolutionary freight and evolutionary potential. This makes the dangers of the transition doubly intolerable, and demands a desperate effort to remove them.

But once we have joined this invisible college, what do we do? Do we join a political party? Picket the White House? Go on protest marches? Devote ourselves to research, education, and propaganda? Or do we go about the ordinary business of life much as we have previously done? Fortunately or unfortunately, according to taste there is no simple answer to this question. Like any other commitment, joining the invisible college of the transition implies a change from the unexamined life to the examined life. What the results of this examination will be, however, and even what constitutes a good grade, is hard to predict for any particular person. What is certain is that we will see and do even old things in a new light and in a more examined manner.

In an earlier chapter we identified the essential problem as that of effecting the survival change in the noösphere. It is a useful question for each one of us to ask, "What changes are taking place in the noösphere, the sphere of knowledge that envelops the globe, as a result of our own life?" We all affect the noösphere in three ways. The content of our own minds is a part of it, so that what happens to our own knowledge and our own images is that part of the noösphere which we can most immediately affect. It is good for all of us to stop occasionally and inquire in what direction the content of our mind is changing, and what the processes are by which this change takes place. We should ask also in what ways do we bring our supposed knowledge to a test—or do we not bother to do this? Do we indulge in any activity which might be described as search—by exposing ourselves, for instance, to unfamiliar sources of information and new points of view?

The second point at which we affect the noösphere is through the information outflow which we make toward others. In conversation, writing, and in the ordinary activity of daily life we are constantly communicating with others, and as a result of these communications their images of the world change. The teacher of course is professionally associated with such an activity, but all of us are teachers whether we like it or not, whether we get paid for it or not, or even whether we are conscious of it or not. The third process is perhaps only an extension of the first. This is the process by which we come to have new knowledge which nobody had before. This process is often regarded as the privilege of a few who are engaged in professional research. The process, however, is not sharply blocked off from the general process of the increase of knowledge in any mind, and a great many discoveries and inventions are still made by people who are amateurs. The more people there are engaged in a search of some kind, who are constantly on the lookout for new and better ways of doing things, the faster will be the general rate of development. The housewife who thinks of a new dish or a new method of resolving disputes in the family, the workman who drops a useful suggestion into the suggestion box, the businessman who pioneers in a new product or method, the government official or politician who develops a new line of policy are all engaged in a creation of new knowledge just as much as the white-coated scientists in the laboratory. The unfinished tasks of the great transition are so enormous that there is hardly anyone who cannot find a role to play in the process.

In a great many areas of life today one sees a certain polarization of the role of the individual, much of which is perhaps quite unconscious but which nevertheless reflects two profoundly different attitudes toward the great transition. On the one hand there are those who despair, who give up hope, and who retreat into nihilism or into the commonplace performance of routine duties. These are the people for whom the pressures and dangers of the great transition are too much, who see so much of the dangers and so little of the potential that they have in effect abandoned the struggle. On the other side are those who still have hope for mankind, who see the enormous potential that lies ahead of us in spite of the dangers, and who therefore seek constantly to build up rather than to tear down, to create rather than to destroy, to diminish the dangers and guide the course. Even among the natural scientists we find some who are concerned with directing their work into significant channels and with playing roles as citizens, others who retreat into a sterile conformity and routine behavior. Among social scientists there are those who are stirred into lively activity both in the pure and applied fields, guided again by the sense of significance of what they are doing and the urgency of man's search for knowledge in this area. By contrast there are others who retreat into sterile methodological dispute or who seek to perform the rituals of science rather than to catch its spirit.

In philosophy there are those who are concerned with new dimensions in the discipline of man's thought, even as they strive with questions that may have no answer, and there are others who relax into a shallow scientism or who erect existentialist despair into an atheistic God. In literature there are those who continue the great traditions by which man uses the exercise of his own imagination to lift himself and achieve self-knowledge—some of these, indeed, are found among the humble writers of science fiction—where others exploit salaciousness in the name of realism and seek to belittle man's image of himself. In art there are those who strive after novelty at all costs and have lost all interest in beauty, and there are those who wrestle with the enormous problem of finding aesthetic standards in a technological age, and who seek to communicate in aesthetic form the enormous danger and potentiality of man's present condition.

In religion there are those who are trying to awaken man to his condition and his modern environment and to develop the great *phyla* of religion in directions which are appropriate to the needs of a developed society. There are others who crudely exploit ignorance in the pursuit of their own power and who seek to give authority to their own prejudices by the invocation of the divine name. In politics there are men who see the necessity for world community and who are engaged within the limits imposed by their own official roles in increasing the probability of peace and the chances of development. There are others who exploit the inner tensions of the masses by projecting hatred on an enemy and who raise themselves to power at the costs of creating disorder and disunion in the world. There are businessmen, managers, and officials who are trying to create humane and workable organizations and to perform the role of the organizer with style and artistry; there are others who are concerned only with minimizing trouble or maximizing gain to themselves. There are housewives and mothers who are raising families of healthy and creative children capable of contributing to a developing world; there are others who are creating neurotics whose value to the society of the future will be negative. There are school-teachers who create in their pupils a sense of the precious-ness of learning and who stimulate their creativity; there are others who use their pupils as outlets for their personal tensions and who kill the love of learning and stifle the creative urge.

One is tempted to end this litany by the good old evangelical hymn and labor song "Which Side Are You On?" This, however, is a dangerous question. It leads to dialectic rather than to dialogue, to preaching rather than to teaching, to self-justification rather than to self-examination, to confirming one's previous prejudices rather than to learning new things. The truth is that each of us is on both sides. The problem is how to raise the one side in all of us and lower the other. I wish I knew an easy answer to this question. Unfortunately I do not. There are many partial answers, but I know no general answer.

The attempt to answer the previous question perhaps leads to another. Is there some point in the great transition at which the invisible college should become visible? Do we need a visible organization like the Jesuits, or the Communist party, dedicated to the ideology of the transition and committed to getting man through it? There is much that is tempting in the idea. It can be argued that the idea of the great transition contains all the necessary elements of an ideology. It has an interpretation of history and an image of the future, a critique of personal and political behavior, and a role for everyone. All that it seems to need is a professional priesthood who will symbolize the idea, propagate it, organize it, and so shepherd mankind into the postcivilized fold. That this is a possible "scenario"—as Herman Kahn* would call it, I have no doubt. But I also have no doubt that it is not the only scenario and I have very great doubt that it is the best one. An elite and disciplined "visible college" looks like an attractive shortcut to the achievement of the ends of an ideology. I think, however, it is a shortcut

* Herman Kahn, *Thinking About the Unthinkable*, New York, Horizon Press, 1962.

which has led in the past almost inevitably if not to disaster
at least to doing more harm than good or, even at best, to
doing good at very high cost. This is an empirical generalization and so belongs to my own definition of folk knowledge rather than to science, and I have to confess that I
have no logical proof that an elite organization dedicated
to what seems a noble purpose always does more harm than
good. Here is an area where genuinely scientific knowledge
has not yet been achieved. I would therefore not rule out
the possibility that in the future we may find ways of organizing a self-conscious society of those committed to the
transition which will not be subject to those temptations,
degenerations, and abuses of power which have characterized all such societies in the past. I furthermore suspect
that such societies are most useful when the ideology which
they propagate contains strong ambivalences. One needs
neither a Jesuit nor a Communist to propagate the multiplication table. I would hope that the concept of the great
transition is more like the multiplication table than it is like
an ideological position. In that case it is better to propagate
it by an invisible college, for the ideas will propagate themselves by their obvious usefulness. They will need very little
of the arts of persuasion or of compulsion. Under these
circumstances a visible society devoted to propagating this
particular truth might well become more of an obstacle than
a facility. For this reason, therefore, I have no desire to plant
a standard other than the truth itself. It is to this that the
wise and honest must repair.

EPILOGUE

By RUTH NANDA ANSHEN

EPILOGUE

EPILOGUE

What World Perspectives Means
by Ruth Nanda Anshen

THIS volume is part of a plan to present short books in a variety of fields by the most responsible of contemporary thinkers. The purpose is to reveal basic new trends in modern civilization, to interpret the creative forces at work in the East as well as in the West, and to point to the new consciousness which can contribute to a deeper understanding of the interrelation of man and the universe, the individual and society, and of the values shared by all people. *World Perspectives* represents the world community of ideas in a universe of discourse, emphasizing the principle of unity in mankind, of permanence within change.

Recent developments in many fields of thought have opened unsuspected prospects for a deeper understanding of man's situation and for a proper appreciation of human values and human aspirations. These prospects, though the outcome of purely specialized studies in limited fields, require for their analysis and synthesis a new structure and frame in which they can be explored, enriched and advanced in all their aspects for the benefit of man and society. Such a structure and frame it is the endeavor of *World Perspectives* to define, leading hopefully to a doctrine of man.

A further purpose of this Series is to attempt to overcome a principal ailment of humanity, namely, the effects of the atomization of knowledge produced by the overwhelming accretion of facts which science has created; to clarify and synthesize ideas through the *depth* fertilization of minds; to show from diverse and important points of view the correlation of ideas, facts and values which are in perpetual interplay; to demonstrate the character, kinship, logic and operation of the entire organism of reality while showing the persistent interrelationship of the processes of the human mind and in the interstices of knowledge; to reveal the inner syn-

It is the thesis of *World Perspectives* that in spite of the difference and diversity of the disciplines represented, there exists a strong common agreement among the authors concerning the overwhelming need for counterbalancing the multitude of compelling scientific activities and investigations of objective phenomena from physics to metaphysics, history and biology and to relate these to meaningful experience. To provide this balance, it is necessary to stimulate an awareness of the basic fact that ultimately the individual human personality must tie all the loose ends together into an organic whole, must relate himself to himself, to mankind and society while deepening and enhancing his communion with the universe. To anchor this spirit and to impress it on the intellectual and spiritual life of humanity, on thinkers and doers alike, is indeed an enormous challenge which cannot be left entirely either to natural science on the one hand or to organized religion on the other. For we are confronted with the unbending necessity to discover a principle of differentiation yet relatedness lucid enough to justify and purify scientific, philosophic and all other knowledge while accepting their mutual interdependence. This is the crisis in consciousness made articulate through the crisis in science. This is the new awakening.

World Perspectives is dedicated to the task of showing that basic theoretical knowledge is related to the dynamic content of the wholeness of life. It is dedicated to the new synthesis at once cognitive and intuitive. It is concerned with the unity and continuity of knowledge in relation to man's nature and his understanding, a task for the synthetic imagination and its unifying vistas. Man's situation is new and his response must be new. For the nature of man is knowable in many different ways and all of these paths of knowledge are interconnectable and some are interconnected, like a great network, a great network of people, between ideas, between systems of knowledge, a rationalized kind of structure which is human culture and human society.

Knowledge, it is shown in these volumes, no longer consists in a manipulation of man and nature as opposite forces, nor in the reduction of data to statistical order, but is a means of liberating mankind from the destructive power of fear, pointing the way toward the goal of the rehabilitation of the human will and the rebirth of faith and confidence in the human person. The works published also endeavor to reveal that the cry for patterns, systems and authorities is growing less insistent as the desire grows stronger in both East and West for the recovery of a dignity, integrity and self-realization which are the inalienable rights of man, who is not a mere *tabula rasa* on which anything may be arbitrarily imprinted by external circumstance but who possesses the unique potentiality of free creativity. Man is differentiated from other forms of life in that he may guide change by means of conscious purpose in the light of rational experience.

World Perspectives is planned to gain insight into the meaning of man, who not only is determined by history but who also determines history. History is to be understood as concerned not only with the life of man on this planet but as including also such cosmic influences as interpenetrate our human world. This generation is discovering that history does not conform to the social optimism of modern civilization and that the organization of human communities and the establishment of freedom, justice and peace are not only intellectual achievements but spiritual and moral achievements as well, demanding a cherishing of the wholeness of human personality, the "unmediated wholeness of feeling and thought," and constituting a never-ending challenge to man, emerging from the abyss of meaninglessness and suffering, to be renewed and replenished in the totality of his life.

World Perspectives is committed to the recognition that all great changes are preceded by a vigorous intellectual reevaluation and reorganization. Our authors are aware that the sin of hybris may be avoided by showing that the creative process itself is not a free activity if by free we mean arbitrary or unrelated to cosmic law. For the creative process in the human mind, the developmental process in organic nature and the basic laws of the inorganic realm may be but varied expressions of a universal formative process. Thus *World Perspectives* hopes to show that although the present apocalyptic period is one of exceptional tensions, there is also an exceptional movement at work toward a compensating unity which cannot obliterate the ultimate moral power pervading the universe, that very power on which all human effort must at last depend. In this way, we may come to understand that there exists an independence of spiritual and mental growth which though conditioned by circumstances is never determined by circumstances. In this way the great plethora of human knowledge may be correlated with an insight into the nature of human nature by being attuned to the wide and deep range of human thought and human experience. For what is lacking is not the knowledge of the structure of the universe but a consciousness of the qualitative uniqueness of human life.

And finally, it is the thesis of this Series that man is

in the process of developing a new awareness which, in spite of his apparent spiritual and moral captivity, can eventually lift the human race above and beyond the fear, ignorance, brutality and isolation which beset it today. It is to this nascent consciousness, to this concept of man born out of a fresh vision of reality, that *World Perspectives* is dedicated.

About the Author

KENNETH E. BOULDING, currently professor of economics at the University of Michigan, received his education at Liverpool Collegiate School and at Oxford. His previous books include *Conflict and Defense, The Skills of the Economist, The Image: Knowledge in Life and Society,* and, with Emile Benoit, *Disarmament and the Economy.*

COLOPHON BOOKS ON SOCIOLOGY